HOW TO ANALYZE PEOPLE WITH DARK PSYCHOLOGY

A Speed Guide to Reading Human Personality Types by Analyzing Body Language. How Different Behaviors are Manipulated by Mind Control

by
LIAM ROBINSON

Congratulation on purchasing this Book and thank you for doing so.

Please enjoy!

© Copyright 2020 by **LIAM ROBINSON**

All rights reserved

No part of this publication may be reproduced, distributed, or transmitted in any form or by any means, including photocopying, recording, or other electronic or mechanical methods, or by any information storage and retrieval system without the prior written permission of the publisher, except in the case of very brief quotations embodied in critical reviews and certain other noncommercial uses permitted by copyright law.

PRINTED IN USA

MIND MASTERY SERIES

SECRET MANIPULATION TECHNIQUES

How Subliminal Psychology Can Persuade Anyone by Applying Dark PNL in Real-Life. Understanding Tactics & Schemes to Influence People and Control Their Emotions

HOW TO SPEED READ PEOPLE

Reading Human Body Language To Understand Psychology And Dark Side Of The Persons – How To Analyze Behavioral Emotional Intelligence For The Mind Control

NLP MASTERY

How To Analyze Dark Psychology Techniques To Change Your Habits And Build A Successful Life. Essential Guide On Mind Control Through Calibrating Emotional Intelligence And Hidden Emotions

EMOTIONAL INTELLIGENCE MASTERY

Discover How EQ Can Make You More Productive At Work And Strengthen Relationship. Improve Your Leadership Skills To Analyze & Understand Other People Through Empathy

*"For better enjoyment, you CAN find all this titles also in audio format, on **Audible.**"*

MY FREE STEP-BY-STEP HELP

I'll send you a free eBook! Yes, you got it right! I'll send you my future projects, in preview, with nothing in return, if you just write a realistic review on them, which I'm sure will be useful to me. Thanks in advance!

Leave me your best email. My staff will send you a copy as soon as possible:

liamrobinsonauthor@gmail.com

Contents

INTRODUCTION TO PERSONALITY ANALYSIS --- 1

CHAPTER 1: HOW CAN I READ PEOPLE? --- 13

CHAPTER 2: THE EYES: THE MIRROR OF THE SOUL --- 26

CHAPTER 3: SIGNS IN DIFFERENT CONTEXTS --- 30

CHAPTER 4: HOW OUR BODY SPEAKS --- 35

CHAPTER 5: VERBAL AND NON-VERBAL BEHAVIOR --- 51

CHAPTER 6: HOW TO SHOW YOURSELF TO OTHERS --- 65

CHAPTER 7: DIFFERENT MOODS FOR SHOWING YOURSELF TO OTHERS ---------------------------------------83

CHAPTER 8: HOW TO MANIPULATE THE PERSONALITY VIA BODY LANGUAGE ---------------------------------92

CHAPTER 9: HOW TO SPOT INSECURITY -------------------------------109

CHAPTER 10: THE INSECURE PERSON IS AN OPEN BOOK! --------116

CHAPTER 11: HOW TO ANALYZE THE TRUTHFULNESS IN A RELATIONSHIP ----------------------------130

CHAPTER 12: HOW THE MIND COMMUNICATES -----------------------142

CHAPTER 13: THE CONSCIOUS MIND --151

CHAPTER 14: THE SUBCONSCIOUS MIND --158

CHAPTER 15: BENEFITS OF PERSONALITY ANALYSIS ------------169

CHAPTER 16: HOW BODY LANGUAGE IMPROVES YOUR MINDSET ------------------------------------171

CONCLUSION ------------------------------188

INTRODUCTION TO PERSONALITY ANALYSIS

Personality screening is a type of assessment that is made to disclose elements of an individual's personality or mental make-up. A personality examination might take the form of a survey or other standardized instruments and can assist in revealing concealed areas of your character enabling you to be familiar with and understand yourself a little better.

According to the American Psychological Association, personality assessment is a 'proficiency in expert psychology that entails the administration, scoring, and interpretation of empirically supported measures of personality traits and styles' to:

- improve professional diagnoses,
- structure and notify mental interventions, and also
- boost the precision of behavioral prediction in a selection of contexts and settings (e.g., scientific, forensic, organizational, academic, etc.).

They have been around since the 1920s and were initially planned to make the process of personnel options much more comfortable. Ever since, they have ended up being widely utilized in other fields, such as connection counseling, career counseling, employment screening, as well as occupational health and wellness.

Personality examinations are psychometric tools that are frequently used in occupation screening. They typically are available in the form of standardized exams whose questions, conditions of administering, structuring treatments and analyses correspond. While an individual's character can be gauged, specific personal qualities, as well as features, and an academic model of personality types can be determined. Not everyone coincides with a particular personality type.

It should be determined if an examination can be relied upon. This is determined through credibility and legitimacy. Legitimacy refers to whether or not it adheres to a specific set of rules. Credibility refers to the degree to which a test creates stable and constant results.

Character tests are strategies created to determine one's individuality. They are used to diagnose emotional issues to evaluate candidates for college and work. There are two kinds of individuality examinations: self-report supplies and projective tests. The MMPI (The Minnesota Multiphasic Personality Inventory) is one of the most typical self-report stocks. It asks a collection of true/false inquiries that are designed to provide a professional account of a person. Projective examinations utilize uncertain pictures or various other unclear stimuli to assess a person's unconscious concerns, needs, and difficulties. The Rorschach Inkblot Test, the TAT (Thematic Appreception Test), the RISB (Rotter Incomplete Sentences Blank), as well as the C-TCB (Contemporized-Themes Concerning Blacks), are all types of projective tests.

A personality test is a method of examining human character constructs. The majority of personality assessment tools (regardless of being freely referred to as "character examinations") remain, in truth, introspective (i.e., subjective) self-report set of questions (Q-data, in terms of LOTS data) steps or reports from life records (L-data, O-data is Observer-report data, T-data is Test data and S-data is Self-report data) such as ranking scales. Attempts to build actual performance tests of individuality have been minimal even though Raymond Cattell, with his colleague Frank Warburton, put together a list of over 2000 separate unbiased examinations that could be made use of in creating impartial character examinations.

One exception, however, was the Objective-Analytic Examination Battery, a performance examination made to measure ten factor-analytically recognized personality trait dimensions quantitatively. Significant trouble with both L-data and also Q-data techniques is that due to thing transparency, score ranges (as well as self-report questionnaires) are extremely at risk to motivational as well as action distortion varying from the absence of sufficient self-insight (or biased perceptions of others) to complete dissimulation (forging right/faking poor) depending on the reason/motivation for the evaluation being carried out.

The first personality assessment measures were developed in the 1920s and were intended to relieve the procedure of personnel selection, especially in the armed forces. Since these very early initiatives, a wide range of character ranges and questionnaires have been established consisting of the Minnesota Multiphasic Personality Inventory (MMPI), the Sixteen Character Variable Survey (16PF), the Comrey Character Scales (CPS), amongst several others. Although prominent, particularly among workers professionals, the Myers-Briggs Type Indicator (MBTI) has various psychometric deficiencies. A lot more lately, many tools based on the Five-Factor Model of Personality have been created, such as the Modified NEO Personality Inventory. However, the Big Five, and associated Five Aspect Model, has been challenged for audit for less than two-thirds of the well-known quality differences in the regular personality ball alone.

Quotes of how much the personality assessment industry in the United States is worth array anywhere from $2 to $4 billion a year (as of 2013). Personality assessment is used in full a series of contexts, consisting of private connection counseling, clinical psychology, forensic psychology, institution psychology, professional therapy, work testing, work health and wellness, and client partnership administration. Personality has a substantial function to play in deciding whether you have the interest and the inspiration that the company is searching for. It additionally figures out exactly how well you are going to fit into the company, in regards to your individuality, mindset and general work style.

In many working circumstances, it's the characters of individuals entailed that influence the day-to-day success of the organization. If a supervisor can't inspire their personnel or the group does not work well together, top quality service, as well as productivity, will suffer.

There have additionally been substantial changes in the past twenty years in the manner in which organizations run. As an example, monitoring styles tend to be less brutal and there are generally fewer levels of monitoring than there were. The relocation in the direction of more database and consumer-focused jobs suggests that individuals have a lot more autonomy within companies. Also, many organizations anticipate going through constant modifications in the manner in which they run to remain competitive.

The companies that generate personality tests as well as the personnel who utilize them invariably refer to these tests as character 'questionnaires' as opposed to 'tests'. This is done to avoid providing the perception that there are right and wrong answers and that the tests can be either passed or failed. No kind of character is always better or even worse than any other. Nevertheless, bear in mind that you are being offered this test for a reason, the company is trying to find something; otherwise, they would not be investing money and time on the screening process.

Why do we do character testing?

Personality testing is beneficial since it:

- Informs us regarding an individual's coping in general as well as with life and tension. In some cases, by producing a stressful scenario in the act of screening, it gives us a possibility to watch the individual react, make sense of something senseless, or react to things and describe their ideas.
- Informs us about just how a person handles details of stressful circumstances or demands, and more concerning exactly how they are taking care of issues now (e.g., severely clinically depressed and self-destructive).
- Can respond to some inquiry propounded us by others, interest in some aspect of work, reach some goal, or chance of a particular behavior.
- Can lead treatment and provide self-understanding for the customer regarding toughness and weaknesses.

What kinds of tests are there?

- **Cognitive tests** are those of memory, intelligence, achievement, etc., you have already researched, and they are assumed to have little to do with individuality although they can.
- **Goal (standard) tests** like the MMPI and Millon take standard inquiries which study shows can aid us to classify people, provide to the patient, and afterward contrast the customer's answers to the solutions offered by specific teams. The MMPI was made to detect clients for psychiatrists, and also the Millon forces individuals right into groups.
- Projective tests are based partially on Freudian suggestions of projection.
  Freud believed we task parts of ourselves we cannot accept. It's a way to get rid of pieces of us we cannot take care of, however, still deal with them. He thought you were, by definition, subconscious of the process.
- Others took the unconscious dismantle, which presumed we project things we can't approve, along with points we can, onto individuals. Thus, what we project informs us something regarding how we believe within. This is more of a cognitive strategy: if you count on the schema, then consider projection as the act of "schematic processing" of details to complete the blanks.

- No matter, we tend to project even more onto things that earn less feeling for us or have less framework for us. The more something is structured, the much less we need to forecast onto it to make sense of it. The more something resembles us, the more we evaluate what we state about it to not think about things we don't want to encounter.

Meehl in 1954 criticized medical psychology for doing way too much with projective examinations and mostly forecasting what we felt onto our clients. He advocated for an actuarial approach to psychology; you obtain billed medical insurance based on your age, sex, area of the country, wellness practices, and so on. We can identify your individuality similarly. This would certainly permit us to develop a diagnosis with better precision and predict actions better. Others slammed this, suggesting that medical diagnosis is not merely picking what an individual resembles outside, but what defines their core. The factor of diagnosis is not only to predict actions but also to predict what treatments will function as well as how. And even regarding precision, disagree like forecasting violence. Research study shows we just aren't that proficient at forecasting it, whatever we do.

Some tests gauge states, or short-term individuality aspects, like the Beck Clinical Depression Supply. Other tests determine attributes or reasonably enduring elements of our personality that can be utilized to predict how we would behave in the future. Some tests are based upon pathology as well as evaluate problems as well as symptoms. At the same time, others are based upon normality as well as assess healthy working and dealing skills. For example, the MMPI examines pathology, while the NEO PI-R evaluates natural characteristics. Ultimately, some examinations are idiographic and contrast your scores on one component to your ratings on another. The Edwards Personal Choice Set Up is like this, based on Murry's ideas of different needs and the weight of some demands over others. Other examinations are nomothetic and contrast your scores to a collection of ratings for "typical" individuals. The Rorschach is one such test.

Some examination styles separate between individuality designs and character attributes. A personal plan is thought to be extra adaptable and less pathological. At the same time, characteristics are viewed as even more stiff and unbending, and more likely to result in significant issues. Numerous character tests examine forging or the purposeful attempt to appear as something other than what you are. There's phony bad, fake good, and fake insane.

CHAPTER 1: HOW CAN I READ PEOPLE?

It's about understanding, beyond words, what other people intend to say. It has to do with sensing what they genuinely mean, even when they say something else. The ability to read people correctly will significantly influence your social, personal, and work life. When you understand just how another person is feeling, you can adapt your message and communication style to ensure it is received in the best means possible. It's not that tough. This might appear magical, but you don't require any type of special powers to recognize precisely how to read people. Below are 17 suggestions for reading individuals like a pro:

1. Be open-minded as well as unbiased.

Before you try to read individuals, you must first exercise having an open mind. Do not allow your emotions or previous experiences to influence your impressions or point of view. If you snap judge people, it will cause you to misread individuals. Be neutral in coming to every interaction and situation. According to Judith Orloff, M.D., "Reasoning alone will not tell you the whole story concerning any person. You need to surrender to various other crucial forms of information to ensure that you can discover the crucial non-verbal, intuitive signs that people release." She says that to see a person plainly, you should "continue to be unbiased and obtain information neutrally without distorting it."

2. Take notice of appearance.

Judith Orloff, M.D., says that when reading others, try to see the individual's appearance. What are they wearing? Are they clothed for success, which indicates they are ambitious? Or they are wearing denim and a t-shirt, which suggests comfort?

Do they have a pendant, for example, a cross or Buddha which shows their spiritual worth? Whatever they use, you can pick up something from it. Sam Gosling, an individuality psychologist at the University of Texas, the author of the guide Snoop: What Your Stuff Says About You, claims that you need to take note of "identification insurance claims". These are points individuals pick to show with their looks, such as a t-shirt with slogans, tattoos, or rings.

Below is a quote from Gosling:

" Identification cases are intentional declarations we make concerning our perspectives, objectives, worths, etc. One of the things that are truly important to keep in mind concerning identification declarations is since these are purposeful, many individuals assume we are manipulative with them as well as we're insincere. Still, I think there's little proof to suggest that takes place. I assume, normally, people truly do wish to be known. They'll also do that at the expense of looking good. They'd rather be seen authentically than positively if it came down to that selection."

Also, some findings recommend that possibly mental attributes can -- to some extent-- be read on a person's face.

Vinita Mehta Ph.D., Ed.M. discusses in Psychology Today:

"Higher degrees of extraversion were related to even more protruding nose as well as lips, a recessive chin, and masseter muscle mass (the jaw muscular tissues used in chewing). By contrast, the face of the people with lower extraversion levels revealed the reverse pattern, in which the area around the nose showed up to push against the face. These searchings for suggestions that maybe emotional characteristics can -- to some degree -- be read on an individual's face, though more research would certainly be needed to recognize this sensation."

3. Pay attention to individuals' positions.

A person's pose says a whole lot regarding his/her attitude. If they hold their head high, it implies they are confident. If they stroll indecisively or cringe, it may be a sign of reduced self-confidence. Judith Orloff, M.D., states that when it involves posture, seek if they boldly hold their head high, or if they walk indecisively or shrink, which shows low self-confidence.

4. See their physical movements.

More than words, individuals reveal their sensations through changes. For example, we lean toward those we like as well as away from those we don't. "If they are trying to lean in, if their hands are out and open, palms up, that's an excellent indication that they are getting in touch with you," says Evy Poumpouras, a former Secret Service agent.

If you have observed that a guy is leaning away, it indicates he is putting up a wall. An additional activity to notice is the crossing of their arms or legs. If you see an individual doing this, it suggests defensiveness, rage, or self-protection. Evy Poumpouras claims that "if somebody is leaning in and all of a sudden you say something and their arms cross, now I understand I stated something that he or she didn't care for." On the other hand, concealing one's hands means that they are hiding something from you. But if you see them biting their lips or cuticle picking, it indicates they are trying to relieve themselves under pressure or in an awkward situation. Understand, of course, that some people bite their lips or pick their cuticles simply out of nervous habit.

5. Try to interpret faces.

Unless you are a master of that poker face, your feelings will be engraved on your front. According to Judith, there are many ways to interpret faces. They are: when you see frown lines created, it might suggest the individual is worried or overthinking. An individual that is giggling will certainly reveal crow's feet -- the smile lines of joy. Another essential thing to watch out for is pursed lips which can indicate temper, contempt, or resentment. Additionally, a clenched jaw and teeth grinding are signs of tension. Affiliative smile: this includes pushing the lips together while likewise making little dimples at the side of the mouth which is an indicator of relationship and taste. Dominance smile: the upper lip is increased, and the cheeks get pressed upwards, the nose wrinkles, an indentation in between nose and mouth deepens, and increased top lips.

6. Don't avoid small talk.

Perhaps you feel anxious with small talk. Nevertheless, it can offer you the possibility to acquaint yourself with the other person. Small talk helps you observe just how a person behaves in typical scenarios. You can then utilize it as a standard to accurately detect any type of habits that are out of the ordinary. In The Silent Language of Leaders: How Body Language Can Help -- or Hurt -- How You Lead, the author (Carol Kinsey Goman, Ph.D.) mentions a variety of errors that people make when trying to read individuals. One of them is that they don't get a standard of just how the other person usually acts.

7. Scan the person's total behavior.

We sometimes assume that if a specific action is done, like looking at the floor during a discussion, it means the individual is nervous or distressed. Yet if you are already accustomed to an individual, you will know whether the individual avoids eye contact or is just unwinding when she or he looks down at the floor. According to LaRae Quy, a former counterintelligence representative for the FBI, "people have various peculiarities and patterns of actions" and a few of these behaviors "can simply be mannerisms". That's why developing a baseline of others' standard actions will help you learn exactly how to determine any discrepancy from a person's habits. You will understand something is wrong when you discover a discrepancy in their tone, speed, or body language.

8. Ask straight questions to get a straight answer.

To get a straight answer, you have to stay away from complicated questions. Always ask outright for a straight response. Remember not to interrupt when the person is answering your question. Instead, you can observe the individual's quirks as they chat. INC. recommends looking for "activity words" to get an insight right into how a person thinks.

9. Make use of notification words and tone.

When you talk with a person, observe the words they use. When they claim, "This is my second promo," they want you to understand that they have already gained a promotion previously. Catch these notification words in your conversations.

10. Pay attention to what your gut tells you.

Listen to your gut, especially when you initially meet an individual. It will give you a natural reaction before you have an opportunity to judge. Let it. Your digestive tract will pass on whether you're at ease or otherwise with an individual. According to Judith Orloff, M.D, "Sixth sense takes place quickly, primitive feedback. They're your interior reality meter, relaying if you can trust individuals." Pay attention.

11. Feel the goosebumps, if any.

Goosebumps happen when we connect with people that move or influence us. It can occur when a person is saying something that strikes home with us. "When we check out research studies [on the cools], beyond the evolutionary feedback to warm ourselves, songs cause it, as well as moving experiences and movies," stated Kevin Gilliland, a Dallas-based scientific psychologist. Also, we feel it when we experience deja-vu, an experience that you have known somebody previously, though you've never met before.

12. Focus on flashes of understanding.

Often, you may get an "ah-ha" moment about people. But remain alert because these understandings can be found in a flash. We tend to miss it since we go onto the next thought so swiftly that these crucial understandings get lost.

13. Feeling the other's presence.

This means that we have to feel the overall psychological atmosphere around us. When you read individuals, attempt to discover if the person has social visibility that attracts you or you face a wall surface making you back off. According to Judith Orloff, M.D, presence is "the general power we produce, not necessarily congruent with words or actions."

14. Observe the individual's eyes.

They claim our eyes are the windows to our souls -- they transmit potent energies. So put in the time to observe individuals' eyes. When you look, can you see a caring spirit? Are they mean? Upset? or safeguarded? According to Scientific American, eyes can "share whether we are lying or telling the truth". They can additionally "act as an excellent detector of what people like" by considering pupil dimension.

15 Don't make presumptions.

This practically goes without saying, however, remember that assumptions lead to misconceptions. When you make presumptions without recognizing the person, it brings a new problem. In The Silent Language of Leaders: How Body Language Can Help -- or Hurt -- How You Lead, (Carol Kinsey Goman, Ph.D.) the writer noted numerous errors people make when checking out others. One of them was not understanding prejudices. For example, if you *think* that your pal will be angry after whatever they claim or do, they will undoubtedly look like they are concealing anger to you. Additionally, do not jump into a verdict when your wife goes to sleep early rather than watching your preferred television program with you. Perhaps she's merely tired -- do not believe she is not anxious to spend time with you. The key to reading individuals like a pro is to relax and maintain an open and positive mind.

16. The technique of watching individuals.

The more you watch individuals, the more you can read them accurately. As an exercise, try to practice watching talk shows on mute. Seeing their faces and actions will certainly help you in understanding what individuals are feeling when they are talking, without having the influence of their words. After that, watch once more with the volume on to see if you are right with your monitoring. This will help improve your technique is an accurate reading.

CHAPTER 2: THE EYES: THE MIRROR OF THE SOUL

Every person knows the expression "the eyes are the mirror of the soul". Yet have you considered its meaning? I recommend contemplating this. Some of the primary sensory body organs are the eyes. With their aid, we see this globe. This is such a familiar process that we start to recognize its significance just by using this capability. Let us turn our thoughts inwards.

It is the eyes that are usually associated with the human heart. Why is that? Perhaps because they cannot lie. Besides, you can deceive with faces and words, however, not with the eyes. The view of a person is, in some cases, so eloquent that it does not call for extra words. It's enough to look at a person in a certain way, and he will undoubtedly comprehend whatever is meant to be conveyed.

A look can be adverse or favorable. Eyes can "smile" or "glow". An individual with this appearance immediately stands out in the group. He can attract others to himself, and motivate self-confidence, since others perceive him as a delighted and kind individual. A brilliant instance is the enthusiast -- their eyes radiate what is impossible to hide.

The sadness of the soul is also inevitably reflected in the eyes. Regardless of how the individual attempts to conceal it, the outside still reflects the inner. Neither a strained smile nor a program of fun can change this. First off, it is needed to heal the soul, to support it, and later, the eyes themselves will betray it. There is still something there - a "glassy look". It is not likely to ever fail to be remembered.

A guy with a vacant appearance is dreadful because his awareness is switched off. His spirit is closed. He is unseeing and aloof.

It can be concluded that the eyes, as it were, are directly attached to the heart and express the deepest variety of sensations and emotions. Taking a look at a person in the eyes, you can understand much about him; it is necessary just to translate what he saw appropriately. Eyes are known to be the mirror of the spirit, the window of the soul.

Cognitive thoughts and feelings are shown in pupil size. Accurate tracking of eye motions can disclose crucial information on psychophysiological steps such as exhaustion.

Your detection is typically needed to establish where somebody is looking. This is of the rate of interest for lots of -- more ordinary -- fields such as advertising, psychology, as well as human-computer communication. Next, to the point of stare, the activity of the eye itself is additionally of interest. When reviewing or checking the environment, the human eye does not stay steady, it moves rapidly and focusses on various fascinating aspects of the visual scene. The motion between one point and another is rapid and cannot be regulated purposely. Such actions are called saccades. The beginning, rate, and amplitude of the eye saccades can offer additional information to psychophysiological values such as exhaustion. Specifically, the paper by Finke et al. shows, how eye saccades connect to fatigue in Several Sclerosis (MS) patients. Both the delayed beginning (latency) of the saccade and the speed is negatively influenced by tiredness. One could, as a result, think about the saccadic latency as an electronic biomarker for exhaustion. The connection between depletion as well as a saccadic lag in the field is presently examined in a test by MS Sherpa.

Professional eye monitoring gadgets make use of unique strategies such as infrared reflections by the retina or electrical signals from ocular electric motor activity to precisely establish eye motions at high temporal resolutions. Applying such techniques in the field is tough. As a result, different methods have been tried to track eyes using ordinary video recordings.

CHAPTER 3: SIGNS IN DIFFERENT CONTEXTS

Conventional signs can have different significances in different contexts or unusual circumstances. The whistle being used by a police officer directing traffic, or a resort doorman mobilizing a taxi, or as the siren of the umpire in a soccer game might all sound precisely the same; their different meanings result from the distinction of context in which the signal happens. They have various objectives as well as being interpreted in different ways.

Etymological signs: Words are linguistic indicators, similar in particular respects to natural and traditional signs. We can review private linguistic indicators – such as names. Still, since we are interested in language usage, and concepts are not generally used alone, we need to direct our interest to entire articulations and how we view, recognize, and interpret them.

Let's think about the issue of understanding, recognition, as well as interpretation concerning language use. To realize what someone states, we need to, first of all, perceive the articulation -- hear a spoken utterance, see a created one. Several points can produce trouble in viewing a word.

Message: way too much sound in the environment, undue distance between the audio speaker and listener, insufficient volume in the speaker's delivery, a weak link if the message is shared by telephone, fixed in a radio message, or not enough attention on the part of the listener. A written word has to be clear, sufficiently lighted, and have the viewer's attention. But hearing alone is not nearly enough, neither is seeing. We obtain no message from an utterance in a language we do not recognize.

Identification of the aspects in an utterance needs audio speaker as well as a listener to share what Clark (1996:92--121) calls 'common ground.' Typically, speaker and listener use the very same vocabulary: they connect the same meanings to the very same words and sentences; they have similar pronunciations; as well as they have, generally, similar ways of putting words together in sentences. Of course, there can be different degrees of commonality in the common ground. Audio speaker, as well as hearer, may speak various languages of the same style so that their pronunciations differ to some extent and there is some aberration in the ways they reveal themselves. One -- or both -- might be a foreigner with only partial mastery of the language they are using. Noticeably different pronunciations, use of vocabulary products that the other doesn't quite understand, significances not shared, syntactic building and constructions not familiar to both -- these disturb the procedure of recognition.

These indicators all 'stand-in' for the suggestion of a tree, as an example. However, they do so in different methods.

We typically classify signs into three types:

Renowned Signs-- icons are indications where significance is based on the resemblance of look. So the drawing of our tree stands in for the notion of 'tree' based upon a crude similarity of look.

Indexical Signs -- Indexical signs have a cause-and-effect partnership between the indicator and also the meaning of the symbol. There is a straight web link in between the two. So a fallen leave could be an indexical indication.

Symbolic Indications -- These indicators have a close or conventional connection. The word tree, t-r-e-e, only involves a stand-in for the notion of a tree because of the conventions of our language. In one more meaning, the symbolic sign for the tree could be 'arbor' (German or Japanese).

In each case, the sign can be gotten into two components, the signifier as well as the represented. The signifier is the thing, item, or code that we 'review'-- so, an illustration, a word, a photo. Each signifier has signified the idea or meaning being revealed by that signifier. Just as they develop an indication. There is typically no inherent or straight connection between a signifier as symbolized -- no signifier-signified system is 'much better' than another.

Language is flexible and adjustable. De Saussure makes use of the word 'arbitrariness' to define this partnership.

An excellent example is the word 'cool.' If we take the spoken word 'cool' as a signifier, what does it represent? In one context or situation, it describes temperature. However, in another, it may refer to something as 'fashionable' or 'preferred'. The partnership between signifier and signified can alter with time and in different contexts.

This is important since signs are understood and described by context. As with the word 'cool,' the partnership between signifier and indicated is made significant in meaning. This area begins by looking at signs in isolation; however, as you become more confident with semiotics, you will undoubtedly start to check out indications as part of a sign system.

CHAPTER 4: HOW OUR BODY SPEAKS

We usually believe we are taking care of things that are going on in our lives okay, yet we discover that our body is giving away the truth of our mind and expressing exactly how it really feels via disease. Condition is specifically that ... Dis-ease of our body and mind.

When you aren't feeling well, despite the disorder, spend some time bent on thought as to what is taking place in your life. It might merely be muscular. But nine times of 10, your body is trying to tell you something. It's sensible that particular organs are affected by certain events. Psychological issues influence the "water functions"; communication issues change the lungs and throat; a concern with the ears -- there's something you either don't want to hear or a person isn't paying attention to you; shoulder discomfort, you are bringing "the weight of the world."

You may wonder just how muscle pressures or broken bones can be linked to your mind? When you think of it, however, it makes sense that if you sprain, turn, or break your ankle joint, it stops you in your tracks. If you've been mostly running around with no time at all to press the time out switch or take time out on your own, you're heading for a fall, and the body is going to take control of you. You might think it's merely a coincidence when it does.

As I mentioned in my first blog online, understanding how your energy is being affected by different factors is critical. At the time, I referred to the power of the moon, and to take this additional action, even more, awareness of what else is happening in your life is a crucial element to accomplishing a healthier balance.

It doesn't always have to be a dilemma that throws your power off balance. A regular day can be filled to the brim with impractical target dates, and there just aren't sufficient hours in the day. Understandably, your body is going to tighten up and act up. "Tightening up" impacts the gastrointestinal system; "not having adequate time" influences the mind, the heart, the lungs -- we feel we can't "catch our breath" we have so much to do.

When we are ill, we most likely turn to medical professionals and get some medicine to make us better; however, in truth, this is merely applying a band-aid over the injury. It's not managing the underlying trouble regarding why you have become ill -- why your body isn't healthy.

As you read this, take a moment to consider what is taking place in your life now. Sit silently and take a time out. Take several deep breaths, shut your eyes and ask your body exactly how it is feeling. Consider your body as something different to your mind and concentrate on that question.

· Do you feel emotions surfacing? Are they delighted or unfortunate?

· Has your power gone down or boosted?

· Has your mind stepped in or advanced the worry that is uppermost in your thoughts or something that you are looking forward to?

Sit silently, focusing on this question, for as long as is comfortable, then list what you heard in your mind or felt in your body. If you felt negative emotions, your energy went down, and a significant concern came uppermost to your thoughts, return to "sitting" and focus on a different question. Ask for recommendations on what you need to do to find a healthier balance.

Recognizing what is taking place in your life to create your body and mind "Dis-ease" is the very first massive action. The next step is to ask your body, your mind, and heart what is it they are trying to tell you that you aren't "getting". Effectively you are attaching to your "higher self" with meditation -- taking time out from "doing" to recognize the problem. A reply might not be rapid, or in the form you expect -- you may wake up in the morning with a "realization"; you might be in the center of your grocery store and even in the middle of the depression when you come to an understanding of the modifications you need to introduce.

You might discover making time to "sit still" the hardest part - besides, you have a lot of "doing" to get done. Yet, as Henry Ford is known to have stated, "If you always do what you've always done, you'll always get what you've always got."

I just recently had a ruptured appendix. As well as I am profoundly grateful for the clinical treatment that saved my life, I recognize that illness is real, that accidents take place, and exactly how medication can help. So I am not writing it to try to convince you that the single reason for your disease remains in your mind, or that you must have done something wrong or are at fault for being ill. Nor am I saying that only by understanding how the brain and bodywork together will you be able to heal on your own whatever it is that ails you. What I am stating is that the function of the mind and emotions in your state of health is a vital one. It is just a part of the overall picture. However, it is the part that is inevitably neglected. By comprehending this relationship, you can recognize yourself more deeply and can assert a more significant role in your very own wellness.

I remember having an upset stomach and pain when I was a kid and my grandma asking me if I was having trouble at the institution. What she knew naturally, we are at last beginning to show scientifically - that there is an intimate as well as a dynamic partnership between what is taking place in your life, with your feelings and ideas, and what occurs in your body. In January 2005, a Time Magazine article showed that happiness, hopefulness, positive outlook, and satisfaction, "show to lower the risk or restrict the intensity of heart disease, pulmonary disease, diabetes, hypertension, colds as well as upper-respiratory infections," while "anxiety -- the severe reverse of happiness -- can worsen cardiovascular disease, diabetes as well as a host of other diseases."

If we separate a microorganism into its part, it cannot function. Each piece has a part to play, even if it is a bit part, so if only one part is malfunctioning, it will undoubtedly affect the whole. Lately, our auto broke down. After it was dealt with, we were informed that it had been just one tiny cable that had actually created the trouble yet the engine cannot work correctly without it. In the same way, if you overlook the duty of your feelings, as well as ideas, you are neglecting one of the most vital parts that make up your whole being. And it might be the one that needs to be dealt with.

Typically talking, we tend to think about our mind and bodies as separate systems as well as think they function, generally, separately. We feed as well as water the body, take it for walks or give it exercise, and appreciate its sensory abilities. Furthermore, we supply the mind with ideas and intellectual searches and amuse it with numerous sorts of activities, while likewise experiencing all kinds of feelings that we generally credit to the means we treat ourselves or just how other people treat us, making us feel either excellent or poorly. When anything fails in any one of these systems, we go to a person to work it out, such as a medical professional to deal with the body or a therapist to treat the mind.

Yet, naturally, we understand that is not the whole story. As an example, can you bear in mind the last time you had a meeting for a task? Or went on a very first day with a person you were genuinely trying to excite? In either situation, no question you tried to appear tranquil and collected; however, at the same time, you were feeling quite awkward and nervous. Can you recall just how your body felt? Self-consciousness will tighten your butt muscles (so you are sitting on your stress), you will sweat more than usual, your stomach may feel somewhat upset. Also, you will probably fluff your words, when you want to appear sophisticated and positive.

Simply put, your emotions influence you physically. However, it could be easy to understand that a frightening idea gets our heart beating quicker. It is more challenging to realize that isolation, unhappiness, or depression can likewise affect us physically. When it comes to complicated feelings or diseases, few people consider our souls to have any relevance. As there are obvious physical causes for illness, such as viruses or accidents, just how can mindset have anything to do with it? Feelings may influence the nerves; however, just how can that have any importance when faced with an illness?

The mind and body are not two but one -- an individual body-mind. Every part of the body is the mind sharing itself via that part. When something fails, it is invariably a mix of both physical and psycho/emotional causes. I am not stating that by understanding the body-mind connection you will have the ability to cure all your physical difficulties. What I am claiming is that such an understanding adds an important, and invariably forgotten, part to your recovery process. By learning the body-mind language of signs and illnesses, you can discover what is being stated or ignored in your psyche and emotions and the effect this is having on your physique. From this viewpoint, you will certainly soon find that there is an extraordinarily intimate two-way communication taking place that influences both your physical state and your mental and psychological health and wellness.

Creating Reliability

Most of us understand the critical demand for a pleasant ambiance in our connections. However, the very same holds true at the office: it requires trust. As I have seen repeatedly in the research I conducted for my book, The Joy Track, a favorable office society is essential for staff member interaction as well as performance. Compassion at the office creates emotional security, which studies by Amy

Edmondson of Harvard shows is produced when supervisors are inclusive and straight forward, and urge personnel to speak out or request help. Mental health improves and efficiency results. A lot more importantly, really feeling risk-free in the workplace assists to encourage the spirit of trial and error that's so critical for advancement.

By utilizing this type of positive, open, and supportive response style, you wind up developing dependability. Equally, as you'll discover, you are specifically conscious signs of honesty in your close companion or friends, employees are particularly alert indicators of relying on their supervisors. Our brains react more positively to empathic managers, as neuroimaging study verifies. In turn, staff members who feel higher trustworthiness show boosted performance.

Preserving a Positive Tone

Positive relationships at work can also reduce health-care prices by enhancing worker health and wellness. Having positive work environment connections strengthens your immune system as well as reduces your heart rate and high blood pressure. Similarly, remaining in a healthy and balanced marital relationship or romantic partnership can increase our physical and emotional wellness.

Leaders and supervisors particularly affect their workers' well-being more than they even understand. A 3,000-person research study discovered that a leader's actions, as well as individuality, also affect their staff members' heart health and wellness. It's no wonder that staff members favor higher happiness at the workplace to higher pay -- which favorable, helpful connections characterize the joy they want.

Compassion

Instead of seeing feedback as "work" or something you need just to survive, see the discussion as a chance to get in touch with another individual who has their own needs and discomforts. Every person, eventually, goes through bumpy rides, depressing times, painful times. By remembering that human experience we all share, you will undoubtedly discover that you can bring generosity and concern into the discussion. Empathy. If you are providing comments, you will probe into what has triggered your employee or co-worker to act a certain way, as well as finding the best words to encourage a different sort of action.

Research study reveals that staff members feel a better commitment and are influenced to function better for supervisors that are compassionate and kind. Again, this is empathy.

Credibility

Despite all these suggestions, you must be genuine, or your efforts will backfire. Just remember how *you* feel when you are around someone who seems to be something they are not -- we often walk away feeling really awkward or controlled. Our blood pressure climbs higher when faced with inauthenticity, according to research by James Gross at Stanford College. You don't want to do that to someone else!

Body Movement

Whether we understand it or not, we are continually reviewing each others' facial expressions and body movements. Picture that you are the person walking into somebody's office to receive responses, or that you are in a meeting. Necessarily, your employer or the job interviewer remains in the position of power. You are most likely paying close attention to their facial expression and nonverbal hints to get an idea of where they are coming from and how they are responding to you. Here are the nonverbal cues to which to pay the most attention:

1. Face. We deduce just how somebody is feeling from their face. Someone's smile turns on the smile muscles in your own face, while their frown activates your frown in response, according to a research study by Ulf Dimberg. We inside register what another individual is feeling by experiencing it in our very own body. Grinning is so vital to social communications that we can discern whether someone is smiling even if we cannot see them. Your smile is, therefore, something to consider, if you are providing comments over the phone. Smile suitably for job warmth and a good reputation.

2. Eye Contact. Research shows the eyes are the windows to the soul. You can naturally understand someone's emotions from their gaze. Eye contact is the vital first step for empathy, the term psychotherapists use to describe an individual's ability to read someone else's emotions. It's also essential for producing a feeling of connection. Make and keep eye contact when you're giving a person comments.

3. Voice. From an early stage, we are acutely knowledgeable about the voices of people we think about crucially. The way we feel regarding another individual affects the way we speak. The tone of our voice, then the words themselves, can express precisely how we think. Brand-new research reveals that we can usually predict somebody's emotions from their voice.

4. Posture. The way an individual sits -- slumped or resting tall, arms open or crossed -- sends a message. When we stroll right into a room and discover someone sitting with their arms crossed, we feel much less connected to them. Having your chest open, arms uncrossed, making sure to maintain nodding, grinning, and articulating (saying things like "mmm" and "yes" in response to the other person's speech) will make you seem interested. Make sure you maintain a non-dominant position, your head and body are lower than the other person, if your position is currently active. The best method for the other person to hear you is if you are not domineering.

5. Breath. Research reveals that the emotions we feel change the way that we take a breath. You have possibly noticed that when you're stressed or angry, you breathe quickly and shallowly, and even when exhausted or frustrated, you are more likely to sigh. Similarly, when we are with a person who sighs a great deal, we may feel that they are frustrated with us.

Before a discussion, try to take some deep, calming breaths. When you exhale, your heart rate and blood pressure decrease, so focus on making your exhale much longer than your inhale. Doing this for a couple of minutes before a meeting will assist you in starting the conference from a place of tranquility. That calmness will additionally help the speechmaker in you to feel much more secure.

6. Focus. Our mind wanders 50% of the time, research suggests. Additionally, offered our active schedules and the messages and e-mails that are popping onto our displays throughout the day, we are not necessarily present with individuals in front of us -- we're still processing something that happened earlier, or we're thinking of a post we recently checked out or a phone conversation we just had.

Focus on the individual you are speaking to right now.
And solely on him.

CHAPTER 5: VERBAL AND NON-VERBAL BEHAVIOUR

VERBAL BEHAVIOR

Spoken habits, additionally called VB or verbal behavior, is a method of teaching language that focuses on the concept that the significance of a word is discovered in its functions. B.F. Skinner coined the term. To educate a child with language delays the importance of a name, one must initially show its purpose. As an example, instead of merely teaching a word, we must teach them exactly how to use those words functionally. For example, a youngster with autism could say the word "toilet" when they see one, however, may not be able to state "toilet" when they require to make use of the washroom or respond appropriately when asked what a bathroom is used for.

Although VBI (Verbal Behavior Intervention) and ABA (Applied Behavior Analysis) are both originated from similar viewpoints, they make use of various methods of teaching language. Some think that VBI is an excellent enhancement to ABA. According to ABA, writing is gotten into components that have different purposes. According to VBI, the first verbal parts of language include choices, mands, tacts, and intraverbals. The term 'mand' describes the youngster demanding or requesting what he needs. This procedure functions as follows: a kid claims apple when he desires an apple. When he is offered a crab, his language is strengthened via getting the apple. This child is likely to repeat this action by having been favorably reinforced, which promptly followed the desired habits. Mostly, the kid is shown to utilize language in a useful means by vocally requesting what he wants and, subsequently, obtaining what he asked for.

With ABA, kids are not necessarily taught to vocally request what they desire, yet to interact it in some way; whether it is verbally, signing, or gesturing, as an example. In the ABA method of training language, children are instructed to label or call points. As an example, they will say the word "phone" when they see a phone. Since they are not always showing the function of the phone, they may not be able to use this word in a sentence. Considering that the focus of VBI is to teach functional language, it can enhance the ABA Discrete Trial approach.

Spoken Habits is one facet of Applied Behavioral Analysis. It is a technique of training communication to individuals that have not yet gotten language. It consists of four "contingencies": Motivational Operation, Discriminating Stimulation, Feedback, and Support (or reinforcement). The last component, reinforcement is essential to ensure the desired skill will undoubtedly be repeated.

History of the Method

In 1957, B.F. Skinner, currently a noted behavioral researcher, composed his book describing several concepts concerning exactly how language is acquired. The guide was criticized since it was not backed up by any type of empirical research studies or experiments; it was merely a set of theories based on observations. In the 1970s, nevertheless, Mark Sundberg, Vincent Carbone, and James Partington started to look more closely into his methods as a technique for treating certain language deficiencies. That led to the advancement of a treatment approach based upon Skinner's propositions. At that time, the treatment, alone or combined with various other methods, had been used to assist lots of people, consisting of autistic youngsters, learn a language.

Just how is it used to teach communication?

The distinction between this technique and the strategies utilized by Anne Sullivan in training Helen Keller is the fundamental reason for making use of words. The Skinner theories suggested making use of inspiration for training language. It isn't just finding out the names of objects, as in the well-known "water, wa-wa" episode, yet finding out the features of the thing named. As an example, if Miss Keller had been parched, as well as her hand had been directed to the water cascading from the pump before she was able to appease her thirst, then "water" would have connected to that met requirement for her. If she had merely found out the name for the fluid, it could not have emerged in her mind as something that could satisfy her demand. She would undoubtedly have been inspired to learn the name for the essential thing to make sure that the next time she was parched, she might interact with her requirement for water.

The trouble with teaching a listing of names of items as well as not linking them to a feature can be described by thinking about an autistic child who has been educated words for the toilet, according to Unique Learning.com. The child recognizes what things are, and can say the item; however, when he needs to utilize it, he may not know just how to use it to meet his needs. That implies he would not advance to using language to ask to use the bathroom.

There are four ideas shown in this method. The very first is "**mand**" or request words. These are instructed to students so that they can **ask** for something they desire. The second is **tact**, or **attention-drawing** names, used to reveal ideas about the thing or to draw attention to it. The third department is **intraverbal** words or words that are used to connect with others, commonly **replying to concerns**, and the fourth is resembling, or **repetition**, which is essential for retention of a concept.

Making use of the four kinds of words, learners are taught to interact verbally and non-verbally. That is, the methods can be made use of to give language to a person who is not verbal. Among the premises of Verbal, Behavior Therapy is that "it is feasible to educate any individual the useful use language."

Advantages of Verbal Behavior

Spoken Habits is an excellent method that can be incorporated with other teaching techniques such as Discrete Test Training (DTT) or Natural Environment Training (WEB). Combining the total operants of Verbal Habits across both DTT and also NET may add to obtaining a complete language repertoire (Sundberg & Michael, 2001). Youngsters require useful abilities across the verbal operants to enhance oral habits, specifically in atmospheres with their peers (Sundberg & Michael, 2001). A youngster without strong intraverbal skills may not interact appropriately in feedback to their peers' verbal habits, which may weaken more interactions. Oral habits additionally profit from the child's motivation, instructing the child to communicate what he needs. This capacity to mand might decrease bothersome actions that worked as a way of obtaining the preferred product.

NON-VERBAL BEHAVIOR

Nonverbal communication (NVC) is the nonlinguistic transmission of details with aesthetic, auditory, tactile, and kinesthetic channels. Numerous channels characterize this form of interaction, and scholars suggest that nonverbal communication can share even more significance than verbal communication. Some scholars say that many people count on certain kinds of nonverbal communication over spoken interaction.

Ray Birdwhistell points out that nonverbal communication accounts for 60 - 70% of human interaction. However, according to other scientists, communication of this kind is not quantifiable nor does it show advanced social interaction when individuals depend a lot on written ways.

The study of nonverbal communication began in 1872 with the publication of <u>The Expressions of the Emotions in Man and Animals</u> by Charles Darwin. Darwin examined nonverbal communication as he noticed the interactions between animals and realized that they expressed themselves through gestures as well as expressions.

These consist of using visual signs such as body language (kinesics), distance (proxemics) and physical appearance, voice (paralanguage), and touch (haptics). It can additionally consist of making use of time (chronemics) as well as eye contact and the actions of looking while talking and paying attention, frequency of looks, patterns of fixation, pupil dilation, and even blink rate (oculesics).

As speech contains nonverbal elements known as paralanguage (consisting of voice quality, rate, pitch, volume, and talking design), in addition to prosodic functions (such as rhythm, modulation, and stress), so written messages have nonverbal components such as handwriting style, spatial setup of words, or the physical design of a page.

Nonverbal communication has can be classified into three principal areas: environmental conditions where disclosure takes place, physical features of the communicators, and behaviors of communicators during interaction.

Nonverbal interaction includes the aware and subconscious processes of encoding and decoding. Encoding is the act of recognizing details such as faces, gestures, and stances. Inscribing information utilizes signals which we may think to be universal. Translating is the analysis of more information from feelings given by the encoder. Deciphering or decoding information uses knowledge one might have of certain received feelings. For example, the encoder holds up two fingers, and the decoder might recognize from previous experience that this indicates 2.

The nonverbal encoding series consists of faces, motions, poses, tone of voice, tactile stimulation such as touch, as well as body language, like when a person moves closer to connect or steps away as a result of spatial limits. The decoding refines the use of received sensations integrated with previous experience into comprehending the significance of interactions with others.

Culture plays a vital function in nonverbal interaction. In numerous Aboriginal American Communities (Native American), for instance, there is often an emphasis on nonverbal interaction, which functions as a valued way by which youngsters learn. Understanding is not dependent on spoken communication, instead, it is nonverbal interaction that works as a critical way of not just organizing social connections, but in conveying cultural worths, so youngsters find out just how to participate in this system from early on.

Social interaction is far more than the explicit meaning of words and the information or message that they communicate. It also includes implicit messages, whether deliberate or otherwise, which are shared with non-verbal behaviors. Non-verbal interaction consists of faces, the tone and pitch of the voice, gestures shown through body movement (kinesics), and the physical distance between the communicators (proxemics). These non-verbal signals can provide hints and additional information and significance over and above spoken interaction.

Types of Non-verbal Communication

The many various sorts of nonverbal interaction or body movement consist of:

Facial expressions. The human face is expressive, able to communicate plenty of feelings without saying a word. And unlike some forms of nonverbal interaction, faces are global. The facial expressions for joy, sadness, anger, surprise, worry, and disgust coincide across cultures.

Body language. Take into consideration how your understanding of individuals is influenced by the way they rest, stroll, stand, or hold their head. The way you move and interact expresses a richness of information to the world. This kind of nonverbal communication includes your posture, bearing, position, and also the refined motions you make.

Motions. Motions are woven into the fabric of our everyday lives. You might swing, point, wave, or otherwise use your hands when arguing or speaking animatedly, typically sharing yourself with gestures without thinking. Nevertheless, the significance of some gestures can be varied throughout societies. While the OKAY sign made with the hand, for instance, conveys a positive message in English-speaking nations, it's considered offensive in countries such as Germany, Russia, and Brazil. But in Japan, it means money. So, it is essential to be careful of exactly how you make use of motions to prevent misinterpretation.

Eye Contact. Since the visual sense is dominant for many people, eye contact is an especially important type of nonverbal communication. The way you check out somebody can communicate numerous points, including the amount of interest, love, hostility, and/or destination. Eye contact is also essential in maintaining the continuation of conversation and also for determining the other person's romantic interest and response.

Touch. We interact a great deal through touch. Think of the various messages provided by a weak handshake, a cozy bear hug, from receiving a pat on the head, or a controlling grip on the arm, for example.

Space. Have you ever really felt awkward during a discussion because the other person was standing so close that they invaded your space? We all require physical space, although how much is required differs depending on the society, the circumstance, and the closeness of the relationship. You can use physical space to indicate several nonverbal messages, including signs of love or affection, and hostility or supremacy.

Voice. It's not just what you say, it's how you say it. When you speak, other people "check out" your voice along with listening to your words. Things they focus on include your timing and pace, how loud you speak, your tone of voice, and even inflection, as well as other communicators such as "ahh" and "uh-huh." Think of exactly how your tone of voice can show sarcasm, anger, affection, or self-confidence.

Just How to Improve Non-Verbal Interaction

Nonverbal interaction is a quickly flowing back-and-forth procedure that needs your complete concentration on the moment-to-moment experience. If you're preparing what you're going to say next, checking your phone, or thinking about another thing, you're sure to miss out on nonverbal hints and fail to recognize the nuances of what's being communicated.

CHAPTER 6: HOW TO SHOW YOURSELF TO OTHERS

We've all heard it: in order to genuinely enjoy others, you need to first learn just how to like yourself. And it's true. Unless you learn to love yourself, you will not be able to let others love you either. The challenge is that these days, our way of living is exceptionally focused on success, comparing ourselves to others, and a desire to do so continually. The result? We have become our own worst critics -- concentrating on our own mistakes and where we "might've done better" than our current successes. So when we hear that real love hinges on our first loving ourselves, we ask ourselves how in the world we're supposed to move from consistent self-criticism to genuine love.

1) What You Need to Recognize First

If there is only one lesson you discover this whole year, it should be this: you are the most important person in your entire world. Your whole life is lived through your eyes. Your communication with the world and those around you, your thoughts, and how you analyze events, relationships, activities, and words comes entirely from you, through you. You may simply be one small person when it involves the grand plan of things, however, when it means your understanding of truth, you are the only person that matters. Because of that, your truth depends upon just how much you love and look after yourself.

Your connection yourself is one of the most specifying considerations forming the type of life you live. The less you like yourself, pay attention to yourself, and understand yourself, the more confused, angry, and even annoying your life will be. However, when you start and continue to love yourself, the more whatever you see, do, engage in, starts to come to be a little bit better in every way feasible. Yet, self-love isn't pure. As they claim, you are your very own worst critic. We're configured to have bouts of self-loathing. For a lot of us, these stages of self-hatred can turn into our whole lives. It's when we invest more time disliking ourselves than we do care for ourselves that we embrace an even more unfavorable disposition of the world. To begin to love yourself initially is invaluable. It might not be the easiest thing on the planet to do. However, it's undoubtedly the most essential.

2) Your Daily You

Consider individuals in your life that you love and regard. Just how do you treat them? You respect them. You are patient with their thoughts and suggestions, and you forgive them when they make a mistake. You provide them with space, time, and opportunity. You make sure they have room to grow since you love them sufficient to rely on the potential of their growth.

Now, think of exactly how you treat yourself. Do you provide yourself with the love and regard that you might offer your closest pals or better half? Do you care for your body, your mind, and your requirements?

Below are the things ways that you could be showing your mind and body self-love in your day-to-day life:

- Sleeping properly.
- Eating a healthy and balanced diet.
- Providing yourself time and room to recognize your spirituality.
- Exercising regularly.
- Thanking yourself and those around you.
- Playing when you require it.
- Staying clear of vices as well as hazardous impacts.
- Showing and practicing meditation.

How much time do you give these everyday activities? If none, how do you enjoy yourself? How do you take good care of yourself?

Loving yourself is more than merely a state of mind -- it's additionally a collection of activities and routines that you incorporate into your day-to-day life. Daily self-care.

You have to show yourself that you love you, from the start of your day to the end. I understand that this easier said than done. However, the primary method I recommend is giving yourself time and room to exercise meditation methods.

I found myself deeply dissatisfied, but I altered my life by submerging myself into the Buddhist viewpoint as well as adopting some fantastic reflection techniques. This is an effective as well as the practical method you like yourself. Via reflection, you'll improve your focus, lower your tension and become familiar with yourself on an intimate level. Via meditation and mindfulness techniques that I utilize every day, I have discovered a way to approve of myself as I am, which is a vital component of caring for yourself and learning self-love. It's complicated, and it will undoubtedly take effort. Yet, if you stick to it daily, you'll eventually experience the benefits that so many individuals talk about with meditation.

3) Accepting the Discomfort

Nobody is perfect. A few of us confuse self-love with limitless positivity and endless optimism. Some tackle their day singing the praises of God no matter how poor they may be feeling or just how terrible their predicament may be. And we believe this is a good thing to do. Shouldn't positive vibes draw in even more positive vibes?

But most of us have a dark side. We all hold distress, disgust, and pain. Let yourself be sincere with who you are.

Forgive yourself for your past actions, those points you are ashamed of. Accept that you occasionally have negative feelings, like disgust, rage, and envy. Acknowledge it.

4) Discover and Open Your Heart

While step 3 has to do with recognizing and acknowledging the discomfort, step 4 is about resolving with a relaxed and open heart. Acknowledging your defects and your faults is one thing, but loving a person that can have your negative thoughts, your bad feelings, your vices, as well as your blunders? That's an altogether higher degree of acceptance.

Discover your life story. Trace your course from childhood years to the person you are today. Understand yourself in the most intimate means possible, and find the reason for every single negative emotion, every shameful act, every word and deed that you are now sorry for. Take the skeletons out of the closet and attempt to keep in mind why they are there in the first place. You are the only one looking. No one can read your mind and see what you are acknowledging only to yourself.

Probably the most critical point you will uncover is that the majority of parts of our character have a cause. Those that don't can be reasoned away. Possibly you have false understandings of truth, or trauma, or feelings of victimhood. Probably you see the world in a different way than it is, and due to that, you made points you currently know to be wrong.

Find the reasons and map your past. Discover to love yourself in a way that only you can. Quit repenting your past and begin understanding it. When you hide away previous feelings, you put yourself in a cage of your own making. The only escape is to push past the unpleasant facts you've been repressing. If you go near the side of the cage, you feel extreme pain. Because of the location of the pain, you can ultimately take care of past injuries as well as the discomfort.

Mindfulness is vital to escape from your mental cage. The more you take care of past emotions through mindfulness the less psychological disturbance can happen. Emotional disruption is based on something that occurred to you long ago, something you have not let go of.

If mindfulness has a lot of evident advantages, why doesn't everyone do it?

This is what I believe: a great many details concerning mindfulness is massive and challenging to comprehend. For instance, advice about thanking deep space or experiencing happiness simply isn't appropriate to many people's lives. And I believe mindfulness -- a functional, realistic technique that every person can exercise -- has been lumped with new-age nonsense like "the law of attraction", "power" and "vibrations". These expressions might seem reasonable. However, they do not operate in truths.

Separate mindfulness from these. They have nothing to do with each other.

5) Share Yourself

On this path of self-discovery, you will undoubtedly uncover truths about you that will horrify and stun you. However, the objective is to push your way through them and face yourself with understanding and acceptance. Only after you have worked out your bumps can you start to see the rough diamond: your present. These are the qualities showing you that survived the journey. The compassion, the spirituality, the humor, the love - every little thing you have earned after cleaning away all the dirt. And when you see yourself and everything concerning you, and accept yourself for who you are, only then can you effectively share yourself with the world. Offer your true self to the world and those around you.

Since you've learned to forgive and like yourself, it's time to start helping others in finding the highest kind of self-love of their own.

6) Your Ideas are Simply Thoughts-- Nothing More

The main thing you should realize is that most of us are naturally adverse. We have thousands of thoughts every day, and approximately 70% of them might be negative. Worries and fears are needed for us to protect ourselves. Yet this survival mechanism can work against us, which is why you're experiencing insecurity and self-criticism now.

So, what can you do?

Well, what you need to realize is that while your thoughts cannot always be changed, you can stop believing them. Ideas are just thoughts -- nothing more. Below is an inspiring quote from Allan Lokos:

"Don't believe everything you think. Thoughts are just that -- thoughts."

7) What Do You Want in Your Life?

Do you have a function?

There is a method. According to Ideapod, these thought-provoking, weird ideas might help you open up to that purpose that has been concealed from you until now.

Check them out:

1. What were you enthusiastic about as a kid?

2. If you did not have to work, how would you choose to fill your hours?

3. What makes you forget about the world around you?

4. What issues do you hold near and dear to your heart?

5. Who do you hang out with and what do you speak about?

6. What gets on your bucket checklist?

7. If you had a desire, could you make it happen?

Remember, if you want to discover just how to love yourself, you need to have an objective that opens that love.

Don't get me wrong, you don't need a life coach or anything expensive. You just need to know your function, your goals, and the steps required to focus your life and move in the direction of a target. From there, it depends on you to act every single day.

If you need a kick-start, have a look at Jeanette Clare's overview on just how to be your very own life coach. She makes use of her experience as a life coach as well as reveals ten actions for you to take control of your life. She supports these actions with vital background information, functional activities, as well as strategies to maintain points both intriguing and interactive. Recognizing what you desire and where you intend to go is essential to being happy as well as search for significance in life.

Keep in mind that your parents loved you before you loved yourself. So self-love does not have to come first. The realization that you are loveable is what is essential. If you believe in a higher power, does not that higher power love you? So you are loveable. You are loved. Now find the way to love yourself.

8) What Are You Pleased About?

Being grateful is an active attitude that can shape your frame of mind for the better. According to Psychology Today, emotionally healthy individuals select to trade self-pity for gratefulness. However, I'm sure you're asking: how do you establish gratefulness to begin with?

According to Unstuck, one of the simplest ways to practice thankfulness is to keep an appreciation journal. Every morning you could write down a couple of points that you're grateful for in your life. Get in the routine, and you'll be much more satisfied every day. Below's a beautiful quote from Roy T. Bennett:

It's only after you've stepped outside your comfort zone that you begin to change, grow, and transform.

9) It's Time to Leave Your Comfort Zone

You have probably heard that progress cannot be made in your comfort zone. It's annoying but true. If you're battling to love yourself, I'm guessing that you're staying in your comfort zone as well. Yet you do not have to do something tremendously scary to get out of there. You can take little actions to move out of it and make progress.

How can you start to move out of that comfort zone? Start to document tasks that make you feel somewhat nervous. Bear in mind, it does not need to be something big. It can be tiny, as long as it's something reasonably new and it makes you somewhat uncomfortable and helps you start knocking those tasks off your list. When you get through them, you'll begin to count on yourself as well as everything that you can achieve.

10) As You Make Progress, People Will Undoubtedly Attempt to Pull You Down

Do you know what takes place when you begin to improve? Your good friends, colleagues, and maybe even relatives may start to pull you down. Why? Because it's the natural order of things. They have placed you in a box, and it tinkers with their minds when you begin to alter it. So you're going to have to summon up some courage and overlook objections from others. If you're becoming sure of yourself and pleased, then that's all that matters.

11) Get Out There and Exercise

You may not like to hear this part, yet it may be among the most important points. Not only will you begin to be much healthier, but you'll feel much better about yourself as well. According to the American Psychological Association, there's usually an immediate mood-enhancing impact about five mins after you begin a workout. When done continually, exercise might help in reducing long-term feelings of anxiety and anxiousness and can help you maintain a healthy and balanced sense of positive self-image.

"There's good epidemiological data to suggest that energetic people are much less clinically depressed than non-active people. And individuals that were inactive and stopped often tend to be a lot more clinically depressed than those who preserve or initiate an exercise program," states James Blumenthal, Ph.D., a medical psychologist at Fight It Out University. So whether it's a cardiovascular workout or weight lifting, go out there and get it done! You'll start to feel much better concerning yourself in no time at all.

12) What Are You Surrounding Yourself With?

This is a crucial step that frequently gets overlooked. We're all influenced by that we invest the majority of our time with. Consider this quote from Tim Ferriss: "You are the average of the five people you spend one of the most time with."

Real, isn't it?

So if you think that a few of your close friends are hazardous and have a practice of putting you down, you might want to find some brand-new ones. Individuals you admire. If your friends support you and are uplifting, you'll begin to feel far better regarding yourself.

13) Accept Your Emotions Without Evaluating Them

Whenever we experience an unpleasant feeling, such as despair, fear, or rage, our initial reaction is to ignore it, deny it or press it away. And this is reasonable. We don't wish to feel psychological pain regularly. When we deny our emotions, we might make things worse. Feelings give us valuable information concerning our lives. A far better strategy that might assist your emotional wellbeing is to exercise acceptance. This suggests failing to assign negative judgment to your emotions. Understand that you don't need to "regulate" your feelings. It is not the *emotion* that damages you. It is what you do to *do away* with the emotion, like consuming alcohol or cake, that can do damage to you. Learning to accept your feelings might actually cause steady emotional durability. However, it is essential not to confuse acceptance with self-imposed suffering. Acceptance is about balance. Western society encourages us to be happy regularly. However, that's not reasonable. Instead, we have to live our lives with both the positive and the negative, trying to keep them in balance. In the end, if you can approve of yourself and all of your feelings, you'll be better able to enjoy yourself.

The better you know yourself and the more well-adjusted you are, the easier it is to step outside yourself, lose yourself, and focus on other people. Without your own issues interfering, you can become objective in your analysis of other people. And that is what this book is all about – analyzing other people.

CHAPTER 7: DIFFERENT MOODS FOR SHOWING YOURSELF TO OTHERS

Hi, there! This is your brain speaking. Just questioning what belief setting you are running in today? Seems straightforward, yet it's essential to understand what's taking place up there. Success in today's hyper-competitive world depends upon what's occurring upstairs in that frontal wattle of your brain where analytic, creative thinking, and various other cognitive features arise. Our study with countless managers and private contributors throughout North America and in 48 other nations suggests that we require three to four times as many suggestions every day to carry out at peak levels in our jobs. Anything less than a continuous circulation of concepts will not be sufficient as we go into a future of constant change.

Fortunately, doing a quick, unannounced check on your thinking mode could not be less comfortable. Use the list here to determine which of the four leading thinking modes you are running in now. Then take a look at the pointers on just how to change your reasoning style.

Defeatist Mode: This psychological state is dominated by worry, irritation, and concern about what might fail. Guess what: we're all propelled into this setting some of the time. In Defeatist Setting, our monkey mind (as the Buddhists call it) feeds us all kinds of the negative and unproductive babble of the gloom and doom range. We're rehashing painful previous occasions and repeating tapes of personal problems and sadness. We dwell on points we "could have, must-have, and would certainly have" done. Defeatist Setting is an adverse use of the creative imagination. Our "idea manufacturing facilities" are shut down, and our idea producing efficiency is stalled.

Sustainer Mode: In this mindset, we're mainly "experiencing the movements," sustaining the status. We persistently examine our tools. We multitask, as well as we grind it out – we're on autopilot. In Sustainer Setting, if a concept does happen to tremble right into mind, we fight to ignore it or invoke reasons it will never work, or will undoubtedly be shot down by managers, spouses, or others. Our voice of judgment - that inner doubter in all of us - is briefly accountable. "Ah, that will never work," or "those in charge would not choose that," or "you have got way too much to do already, you can't possibly find time to do something with that," are all indications of this frame of mind. From a performance viewpoint, this setting is an inescapable part of life. Many tasks are primarily regarding implementation and adhering to recognized plans, treatments, and methods. The downside of investing extended periods in this mode is that it can numb and diminish creative thinking, rather than forcing us to challenge the status quo with mind-altering suggestions.

Daydreamer Mode: If this is your mindset today, kiss your mind! You get on a performance course, at the very least as far as creating ideas is concerned. Something has promoted those endorphins of dreaming, and it is essential to determine what. Perhaps you took a small walk in nature or had an enjoyable conversation with a good old friend that genuinely listens to you and is encouraging. Maybe you got some excellent news that set you off in a positive direction. In Daydreamer Setting, you create suggestions conveniently and without too much initiative -- lots of them. You have ideas like "wouldn't it be fantastic if." Useful MRI brain scans reveal the brain's satisfaction facilities illuminating when we're in this state.

Opportunity Setting: In this setting, our suggestion factories are running at peak performance degrees. Possibility Mode builds upon the Daydreamer Mode, but there's an added aspect: an action-taking part. You are not content simply to hatch concepts -- you have objectives to make those desires a reality. Given that innovation is not only coming up with ideas, but additionally bringing them to life, the disadvantage of Daydreamer Mode is that we never carry out, never actually enjoy the rewards of completing, or of performing at peak degrees.

When Martin Luther King informed the crowd "I have a dream" from the steps of the Washington Monument, he had not been merely fantasizing. This was the visual personification of a man in Opportunity Setting, and his speech altered the course of history. Opportunity Setting is an individual, positive, glass-is-half-full, can-do mindset. Your mindset is of unbridled excitement; you're willing to attempt anything and everything until you make it. Problems turn into opportunities. Barriers are simply difficulties to be overcome. The difficult simply takes you a bit longer.

Just How to Change Settings and Elevate Performance

As an innovation train, a big part of my task is helping clients a) become conscious of their primary mode, and also b) discover strategies for consciously changing their setting to unleash the Opportunity frame of mind. Right here are four tips on exactly how to take charge and shift settings:

1. **Regularly Check Up on Your Mode of Thinking.** The terrific personal motivation trainer and audio speaker Zig Ziglar suggested "a check-up from the neck up." The most vital dialogue you'll have today is with yourself. As you drive home from your job, ask yourself, "What mode of thinking have I been running in today? In current days? What's my self-

talk been, and why?" What adjustments to your external environment might you make to coax you into Opportunity Mode in of the moment?

2. **Act On an Idea**. Have a look at your "things to do" checklist. Pick one out and make it happen! Activity relieves worry, cures inertia, and can alter an adverse frame of mind. The contentment of accomplishing - even a little task - or eliminating an irritant can bring about more activity, perpetuating itself into a virtuous cycle. There's nothing more enjoyable than striking off an item on the typical "to-do" list and here's why: it changes your mental model from Defeatist/Sustainer to Dreamer/Doer.

3. **Count to 10 and Win**. To shift out of Defeatist Mode, virtually count your blessings. List all the things in your life you have going for you: your buddies, job, belief in a higher power, and so on. To change from Sustainer Mode to Opportunity Mode, help yourself to find as many answers as possible to a challenge or issue you presently face. Essentially, force yourself to tap into that part of your brain: What are ten ways you might address this problem? What are the ten reasons that you are happy to be alive? After you've shown yourself that you can do this, think about how you can help others in jumpstarting their reasoning and change into efficiency-boosting mode.

4. **Let Your Dreamer Mode Come Out to Play.** Among my favorite techniques is WIBGI, which means "Wouldn't It Be Great If..?" To assist yourself or your associates, shift to a much more visionary mindset. Invite individuals to weigh in with statements beginning with: "wouldn't it be great if" then pronounce whatever comes to mind. "Wouldn't it be great if…we could eliminate this resource of client complaints at last?" "Wouldn't it be wonderful if…we could halt business e-mail after 6 pm and before 8 am?"

   To use this technique, invite individuals to think about a customer irritant, a job, a policy, item, or procedure that requires an upgrade. Then take a step back and take a look at exactly how doing this will change the predominant way of thinking.

It's easy to fall into the less productive way of thinking without being aware of it. It's an unavoidable part of human existence to sometimes operate from the Defeatist or Sustainer Modes. But in recognition there is power. Become self-aware and identify when you remain in a harmful setting and use the above strategies to overcome and change. Opportunity Mode is what you're in search of; it's where efficiency originates, is considerably increased, and it's where your concepts flow like a mighty river. Strive for it as often as possible.

CHAPTER 8: HOW TO MANIPULATE THE PERSONALITY VIA BODY LANGUAGE

Body movement refers to the nonverbal signals that we utilize to express ourselves – whether consciously or unconsciously. According to specialists, these nonverbal signals compose a big part of everyday interactions. From our faces to our body language, things we don't say can still share volumes of information. It has been said that body movement may account for between 60 - 65% of all interactions. Understanding body language is essential. Yet it is still necessary to take note of other hints such as context. You need to take understand signals en masse as opposed to concentrating on a single activity.

When we talk about body language, we look at the refined hints we send and give to each other non-verbally. Many people would like to know how to interpret body language. To get going, body language can be broken down into a couple of various types.

Watch the Eyes.

The eyes are regularly described as the "windows to the soul" given that they are capable of disclosing a great deal concerning what an individual is feeling or believing. As you talk with another person, taking note of eye activity is a natural and vital part of the interaction process. Some usual points you may observe include whether individuals are making direct eye contact or averting their look, just how much they are blinking, or if their pupils are dilated.

When assessing body movement, take note of eye signals. Eye movements can be very informative.

When it concerns eye habits, it is also suggested that looking upwards and to the right during discussion shows a lie has been detected while looking upwards and to the left indicates the individual is telling the truth. The reason for this is that individuals lookup and to the right when using their creativity to concoct a story and search and to the left when they recall a real memory.

Eye Contact: When interacting with a person, take note of whether she or he makes direct eye contact or averts them. Lack of ability to make direct eye contact can suggest boredom, disinterest, and even deceit -- especially when someone looks away and sideways. If an individual overlooks, on the other hand, it usually shows anxiety or submissiveness.

When a person looks directly into your eyes while having a discussion, it shows that they are interested and paying attention. Nevertheless, extended eye contact can feel harmful. On the other hand, breaking eye contact and often looking away could indicate that the person is sidetracked, unpleasant, or trying to conceal his/her real feelings.

Blinking: Blinking is all-natural, but you also need to take notice of whether a person is blinking way too much or insufficiently. People frequently blink more swiftly when they are feeling distressed or uneasy. Random blinking might show that an individual is purposefully trying to regulate his or her eye activities.

An individual's blinking rate can speak volumes about what is taking place internally. Blink rate increases when people are thinking more or are worried. In many cases, increased blinking frequency shows lying -- specifically when accompanied by touching the face (particularly the mouth and eyes). Glancing at something can suggest a need for that thing. For example, if somebody eyes the door, this may indicate a need to leave. Eying an individual can indicate a desire to talk with him or her.

Pupil Size: Pupil size can be a subtle nonverbal interaction signal. While light degrees in the environment control pupil expansion, sometimes emotions can also cause small changes in pupil dimension. For example, you may have heard the phrase "bedroom eyes" used to define the look somebody gives when they are attracted to another person because highly dilated eyes suggest that a person is interested and even excited.

Additionally, dilated pupils determine if somebody is responding favorably towards you. Pupils expand when cognitive initiative increases, so if somebody is concentrated on someone or something they like, their pupils will instantly dilate. Pupil dilation can be challenging to see; however, under the appropriate conditions, you ought to be able to spot it.

Facial Expressions.

Although individuals are more likely to regulate their facial expressions, you can still detect vital nonverbal signs if you pay attention.

Mouths can be significant. Grinning is a crucial nonverbal hint to look for. There are different types of smiles, including real laughs as well as fake smiles. An authentic smile suggests that the individual enjoys and appreciates those around him/her. A fake smile is indicative of enjoyment or approval but suggests that the smiler is feeling something else. A "half-smile" is another typical facial habit that only involves one side of the mouth and suggests mockery or uncertainty. You might likewise notice a minor grimace that lasts less than a second before somebody smiles. This generally indicates that the person is concealing his or her frustration behind a phony smile.

Limited, pursed lips additionally show displeasure, while a kicked back mouth indicates a loosened up attitude and favorable state of mind.

Consider, for a moment, just how much an individual can share with just their face. A smile can indicate reassurance or joy. A frown can signal displeasure or heartache. Sometimes, our faces may express our real feelings about a particular scenario.

Just a couple of examples of emotions that can be shared through faces include:

- Happiness.
- Sadness.
- Rage.
- Shock.
- Disgust.
- Fear.
- Confusion.
- Excitement.
- Ridicule.

The expression on an individual's face can even help establish whether we trust or believe what the person is saying. One research study found that the most reliable face included a slight raising of the brows and a mild smile. This expression, the researchers say, conveys both kindness and self-confidence.

Scientist Paul Ekman has discovered support for the universality of a range of facial expressions tied to specific feelings consisting of joy, temper, concern, surprise, and despair. The study also suggests that we make judgments about an individual's knowledge based upon their facial expressions. One research study showed that people that had narrower faces and more prominent noses were most likely to be regarded as intelligent. Individuals with smiling, happy expressions were likewise evaluated as being smarter than those with angry expressions.

The Mouth.

Mouth expressions and activities can additionally be valuable in reading body language. For instance, chewing on the bottom lip may indicate that the individual is experiencing feelings of concern, anxiety, or insecurity. Covering the mouth might be an initiative to be respectful if the person is yawning or coughing, yet it may likewise be an attempt to cover a frown of displeasure. Grinning is maybe one of the most significant body language signals, yet grins can be interpreted in several other ways. A smile might be real, or it may be used to reveal false happiness, mockery, or even resentment.

When evaluating body movement, take notice of the mouth and lip signals.

Pursed Lips: Tightening the lips could be an indication of distaste, displeasure, or question.

Lip Biting: People often attack their lips when they are stressed, nervous, or stressed out.

Treatment of the Mouth: When individuals wish to hide an emotional reaction, they may cover their mouths to avoid showing smiles or smirks.

Shown Up or Down: Slight adjustments in the mouth can also be refined indicators of what an individual is feeling. When the mouth is somewhat turned up, it may suggest that the person is feeling happy or hopeful.

When lips are swollen so no creases are seen, this, too, can be a sign of interest – even sexual interest. Watch for this reaction then determine whether it is interest in you personally or in your business proposal.

Gestures.

Motions can be one of the most straight and visible body language signals. Swing the arms, aiming the fingers, as well as using the fingers to suggest numerical amounts are all very typical and understandable gestures. Some gestures might be social, so providing a green light or a peace sign in another country could have an entirely different meaning than it carries in the United States.

The following are a few typical gestures and their possible definitions

- A clenched fist can suggest temper in some circumstances or solidarity in others.
- A thumbs-up, thumbs down, are commonly used as gestures of authorization and displeasure. But in the Middle East, it's akin to giving someone the middle finger in the United States. In Bangladesh, thumbs up is taunting someone into a fight.
- The "alright" gesture, made by touching together the thumb and the forefinger in a circle while extending the various other three fingers, can be used to imply "okay" or "all right." In some parts of Europe, however, the very same signal is utilized to indicate you are nothing, as in a big fat zero.
- The Vindication, developed by raising the index and middle finger in a V-shape, indicates peace or victory in some countries. In the United Kingdom and Australia, (and various other countries) the icon has an offending definition when the palm is facing the person giving the sign.

Analyze the Setting of the Arms.

Think about a person's arms as the entrance to the body and the self. If a person crosses their arms while engaging with you, it is typically viewed as a defensive, obstructing gesture. Crossed arms can also show anxiousness, susceptibility, or a closed mind. If crossed arms are accompanied by an authentic smile and relaxed posture, then it can show a confident, kicked back attitude. When a person puts their hands on their hips, it is usually utilized to indicate supremacy, usually by men more often than women.

The above suggestions can provide you understanding of the true objectives behind a person's actions, yet it is not absolute. When analyzing body movement, remember that these methods will certainly not relate to all individuals, 100% of the time. Specific variables such as culture and an individual's general body language should be considered to more precisely translate non-verbal hints. The more you practice analyzing body language, the more you will correctly recognize the signals.

Recognize Hand Signals.

As with the arms, the hands leak vital non-verbal signs when looking at body language. This can show anything from uneasiness to straight out deception. Subconscious aiming indicated by hand motions can also speak volumes. When making hand gestures, an individual will motion in the direction of the person they are fond of (this non-verbal hint is especially vital to watch for during conferences and when interacting in groups). Supporting the head with the hand by relaxing an elbow on the table can show that the guy is listening and is holding the head still to concentrate.

Supporting the head with both joints on the table, on the other hand, can indicate dullness. When a person holds an item in between him or her and another person they are communicating with, this acts as an obstacle that is indicated to block out the other person. As an example, if two individuals are speaking and someone holds a writing pad in front of him or her, this is thought to be a blocking act in non-verbal interaction.

Where Do the Feet Point?

A part of the person's body where people often "leak" essential non-verbal hints is the feet. The reason people inadvertently send non-verbal messages through their feet is that they are generally so focused on managing their faces as well as the top of their body that they forget about their feet. When standing or resting, an individual will generally point their feet in the direction they wish to go. So if you notice that a person's feet are aimed in your direction, this can be a great indicator that they have a favorable opinion of you. This points to one-on-one interaction as well as group interaction. You can tell a whole lot concerning team dynamics just by examining the body movement of the people involved, which means where their feet are pointing. Also, if somebody is talking with you, yet their feet are pointing in the direction of someone else, likely, she or he would rather be speaking with that person (no matter if the top of the body cues suggesting something else).

Observe Head Activity.

The speed at which an individual nods their head when you are talking suggests their patience -- or lack thereof. Sluggish nodding indicates that the individual is interested in what you are saying and desires you to continue to chat. Rapid nodding shows the person has listened to enough and desires you to finish talking or provide him or her a chance to speak. Tilting the head laterally throughout the discussion can be a sign of interest in what the other person is claiming. Tipping the head in reverse can be an indicator of uncertainty or unpredictability. Individuals additionally aim with the head or face at people they are interested in or share a fondness with. In groups as well as conferences, you can tell who the people with power are based upon how many individuals consider them. On the other hand, less-significant people are noticed much less commonly.

Take Notice of Closeness.

Distance is the range between you and others. Take note of exactly how close someone stands or sits to you to determine if they view you favorably. Standing or sitting close to a person is possibly one of the best indicators of connection. On the other hand, if someone stands or moves away when you come close, this could be an indicator that the connection is not shared.

You can tell a lot about the sort of connection two people have just by observing the distance between them. Remember that some societies favor more or less range during an interaction, so closeness is not always an accurate sign of affinity with someone. Consider where you are and the nationality of the people involved when assessing a situation.

Consider Mirroring.

Mirroring entails copying another's body language. When communicating with somebody, check to see if the person mirrors your actions. As an example, if you are sitting at a table with a person and rest an elbow on the table, wait a few seconds to see if the other individual does the same. Another usual mirroring gesture entails taking a sip of a beverage at the same time. If a person mimics your body language, this is an excellent indication that she or he is trying to develop a rapport with you. Try altering your body position and see if the other person adjusts theirs similarly. These can even go as far as mimicking your breathing pace.

Are you enjoying this eBook, or have you found it interesting up until now?

*Your support really makes a difference! I would be very grateful if you would publish an exhaustive review on **Amazon**. All reviews are read personally so that I can get real feedback and make this book (and the whole series) even better.*

Thanks again for your support!

CHAPTER 9: HOW TO SPOT INSECURITY

"When ideas come to be action -- that is where it begins to break down," Caleb Backe, health and wellness professional at Maple Holistics, tells Bustle. "Being rather troubled or a little jealous/paranoid is all-natural. We can be controlling, often without even implying it. You can think about all kinds of things, and it doesn't necessarily guide your choices. Yet this changes when you begin acting upon your insecurities. If you do not keep your insecurities in check, you may end up losing your partner."

Put simply, if your insecurities are triggering you to believe negative thoughts, which later materialize into unfavorable activities, that's when your partnership can begin feeling several of the adverse effects of your insecurity. It might not take place overnight. Yet understand that it's OK if you need to overcome some insecurities, whether that's on your very own, with a therapist, or with the love and support of your companion. Below are seven signs that your instabilities are influencing your connection, according to professionals.

Instability comes from our concern of 'not having sufficient' or 'not being enough'. These anxieties are vanity based. When we are unconfident, we bother with what others think about us and also do not have a strong feeling of self and even healthy self-worth. Here are a couple of indications of instability that can indicate you need to lock out the voice of the ego and be true to on your own.

1. Boasting

One of the most usual indicators of instability is boasting regarding what you have and what you have attained. Troubled individuals often try to thrill other individuals. They are hoping for recognition from the exterior world. If you have a positive sense of self, you don't feel the requirement to excite others regularly. You certainly do not need other people to validate you. So if you see someone boasting about themselves, you are probably seeing a very insecure person.

2. Controlling

Individuals who are controlling can occasionally appear to be stable. Nevertheless, controlling behavior originates from anxiety and also insecurity. It is just one of the most common indications of instability. When we are afraid that we may not be able to deal with what life throws at us, we attempt frantically to control the world around us as well as keep it within appropriate boundaries so that we feel risk-free and safe and secure. This can lead us to control other people if we can just to feel safe so they act in foreseeable ways. When we understand that we can handle life, whatever happens, we no longer feel the demand to control every little thing to feel rigidly secure. We can then start to go with the flow and delight in life in all its messy glory.

3. Stress and Anxiety

Anxiety comes from so many sources. Often, it originates from a sensation of not being good enough. Frequently when we are anxious, we are afraid of what other people may think of us, or we are so scared we will ruin something in some way.

Individuals that are secure in themselves don't often feel anxious. This is since they do not put so much emphasis on always being right. Although they might still establish high requirements for themselves, they do not beat themselves up for every mistake. They understand that they are only human and that they will undoubtedly get things wrong sometimes and that's okay.

Feelings of anxiety can often signify insecurity. Clinical depression can happen when a buildup of tension triggers you to pull back from life. We often take our stress out on the world to ensure that we won't get injured or criticized or won't fall short. By developing a strong feeling of self, you can venture right out into the world without a lot of anxiety. Of course, stress is not always straightforward to recoup from. However, small acts of self-kindness and being mild with yourself is an excellent way to start to move out of crippling clinical depression.

4. People-Pleasing

A clear sign of instability is the overzealous demand to please other individuals at all times. This hinders living your own life. It can occasionally seem like your life does not belong to you when you are always trying to make others happy.

People with high self-esteem show caring and empathy for others but do not feel they are accountable for other people's happiness. And that is real. You are exempt from other people's satisfaction, and you do not need to secure or rescue them from every unpleasant thing they might experience.

If you are a people-pleaser, you must make time in your life for yourself. You must do the things that make you happy and follow your own desires and not merely assist others in accomplishing theirs. However, people-pleasing can result in bitterness and even a feeling of martyrdom. This is not a healthy and balanced method to be. People-pleasing is terrible for you as well as it is bad for others as it is often harmful to their personal growth.

5. Perfectionism

If you feel like nothing you do is good enough, or you spend an excessive amount of time making everything 'perfect,' this may signify insecurity. This typically boils down to a fear of failure or criticism. You find it tough to move on from a job since you fear the outcome may not be what you hoped. Regrettably, this can result in you getting stuck, never being able to finish things, or investing too much time on whatever you do. This can cause you to stop working to meet due dates or let people down. This harms your self-esteem and can be a downward spiral. Perfectionism can be tough to escape from, but having a healthy and balanced feeling of self-worth, and being kinder and more accepting of who you are is a place to start.

When you are analyzing other people, watch for these above signs in them. Are they boasting? Trying to control or manipulate the situation? Are they stressed or anxious and showing signs of it? Can you detect signs of people-pleasing or perfectionism in their actions? Noticing any or all of these signs can help you to analyze a person quickly and have insight into them just as though you are reading their mind.

CHAPTER 10: THE INSECURE PERSON IS AN OPEN BOOK!

What About a Man?

Guys are not that complex. Their needs and their inhibitions, their hopes and their dreams only take 204 pages to explain in What Men Want as well as to turn to your advantage, a book which has stuck around consistently around the top of the numerous best-seller lists since it arrived on the American market in 1998.

Writers Bradley Gerstman, Christopher Pizzo, and Richard M. Seldes explain themselves as "three regular people" that "give females an uncommon yet straightforward look inside men's minds". The Regulations from a guy's point of view, simply put. It would seem the discerning American woman remains in deep turmoil about her menfolk. And the book promises to inform the stunned woman regarding "what he means when he claims 'I'll call you',". It also discusses "why some guys cheat on the lady they love" all shown in a tempting, page-turning formula.

As Christopher Pizzo himself informed The Irish Times from his Manhattan accountancy firm, males have been getting a guide for their womenfolk - so now the picture is painted of what males want females to know they desire. Pizzo has no doubts claiming what he and his two white-collar co-authors ("Brad's a lawyer and Rich is a medical professional") want is what every guy wants. "Guys," he explains, "are not all that complicated."

Gilford D'Souza, an expert counselor and connection therapist at the Awakenings Centre in Rathfarnham, Dublin, defines this guide as "really valuable for any person who is trying just to get to the stage of dating and beginning a partnership. Yet it fails in informing you exactly how to go from there. It goes into no detail concerning exactly how to keep a partnership going."

Though ostensibly a publication concerning what guys want, he claims, it is a book regarding guys' insecurities.

"Women have substantial power over guys. Just like women, guys have a massive fear of rejection, but there is a stress on them to appear brave, to ignore those feelings. Usually, too, they are much less likely than ladies to be in touch with their own sensations. Males require security, love, and understanding, in addition to a feeling of freedom and male bonding."

So, it appears males want mollycoddling females that will at the same time indulge their every whim to go out with the lads. The writers inform us: "We need to hang out with other men. Male bonding is one of the most treasured routines for males ... it's more to him than just a simple evening out. It is his time to be a guy amongst guys."

In a chapter on "The First Date": "Ladies are amazed when we tell them what several professional males look for in a lady on the very first date. Guys like women that behave. Men are suckers for compassion, a factor to consider. Understand how a male feels on a first date. We are stressed that the beverages aren't sufficiently cold, that the food won't suffice. We stress that she doesn't like our choice of restaurant, or that she doesn't like us."

The Big 5 Personality Characteristics

Typically speaking, psychology holds that five significant variables, or characteristics, shape our personalities: openness to experience, conscientiousness (self-control to advance), extraversion (being friendly), agreeableness (consisting of being mindful of others), and neuroticism (subject to worry). Each of these "big 5" has six dimensions. If you resemble me, you most likely appreciate taking those cost-free online examinations to see where you fall on each.

It's probably instantly apparent that our characters shape our reactions to things that take place with us. Somebody that is agreeable is going to make an effort when an unexpected visitor pops by, for instance. Yet variations in our characteristic might likewise indicate we may experience the world in different ways than others do.

Consider being "unbiased." In an experiment, Luke Smillie, psychotherapist and director of the Character Processes Laboratory at the College of Melbourne in Australia, and his colleagues discovered that individuals that score higher on that personality attribute "may essentially see the world in different ways from the typical individual." Their minds perceive information that others strain, aiding to drive imaginative reactions. Find out more below regarding the study in Smillie's article, "Openness to Experience: The Gates of the Mind."

Some people are open books; they share themselves with others without the anxiety of what the consequences could be. They aren't capable of staying bottled up, and so they believe in expressing their thoughts and feelings honestly. For others, it is wearisome to reveal themselves, and so they are somewhat the reverse of an open book. Right here is just how readable you are, based upon your personality type.

Myers-Briggs Personality Type Indicators

INFJ

INFJs are closed books, quite the contrary in many situations. They have many layers; it commonly takes a long time for them to peel those layers back and reveal themselves to another person. They are generally creative, caring, and gentle as well as introverted.

ENFJ

ENFJs aren't usually open books either, considering that it feels awkward for them to open up to others fully. They don't find it easy to share a lot of specific things with others even though they have a method of making it seem like they are more open than they are. Instead, they take some time to feel like they can trust someone sufficiently to reveal their thoughts and feelings to them or their worries. They're also warm, extroverted, and tolerant.

INFP

INFPs are introverted so they won't share themselves well, and this is simply naturally who they are. INFPs frequently place their hearts on the line, but this is simply who they are. The INFP is a thoughtful, introverted, daydreaming mediator.

ENFP

ENFPs are typically open books the majority of the time, given that they feel a lot comfier sharing themselves. This 'campaigner personality' is quite extroverted. They want to share their ideas and sensations, and themselves. For the ENFP being an open book just implies being themselves as well as sharing what is taking place inside of them. They could have some points they don't feel as open with, yet the majority of the time ENFPs are open. They're curious and constantly exploring new ideas with their intuitive and active personalities.

INTJ

INTJs are not open books; rather, they are typically individuals that keep things secured tight. These introverts don't find it natural or straightforward to reveal their feelings to others. INTJs don't easily trust people, and so they don't find it natural to subject themselves to others. They are intuitive, rational, thinking types.

ENTJ

This is the Commander Type. ENTJs can be open books since they are extroverted. They like to be in charge as they feel more comfortable focusing on facts and even logic. Therefore their feelings can be neglected quite a bit.

They're thinking and judging personalities lead to moments and accomplishments.

INTP

INTPs are usually the reverse of an open book because of their introversion and typically take a long time to feel comfortable around someone. They will undoubtedly reveal parts of themselves when they do trust a person. However, it takes time for them to open up if they truly feel safe doing so. They can have trust issues. Even though these personality types are logicians, they are flexible thinkers who may take the creative path with an unconventional approach in many aspects of life.

ENTP

The Debator Personality is extroverted and therefore easily readable. The personality is charismatic. He's focused and ideas and concepts rather than facts and logic making him rarely boring. He is energized by spending time with other people. And will probably energize you as well.

ISTJ

Not only is the ISTJ introverted, and therefore a closed book, he's observant so he's going to be watching you – reading *your* book. These are honest people with strong family values. They're responsible organizers – neat and orderly – good at running systems and institutions, heads of households. They are reserved, practical, and quiet and won't be revealing themselves to others any time soon. They look for peace in both their private lives and their professional lives. You can rely on them as both friends, lovers, and co-workers. Search out the ISTJ.

ESTJ

This is the Executive Personality. ESTJs aren't open books a lot of the time and frequently find it difficult to open themselves as much as those around them despite being extroverts. These traditionalists value honesty. They are dedicated hard works who take charge. Orderly and rule-abiding, this is the personality type you can put in charge of your business.

ISFJ

This is the Defender Personality. Although they can be assertive, they are introverted and observant which keeps them from laying their feelings on the line. Their empathic personality helps them be supportive of others. They are unassuming caretakers who are loyal, practical, compassionate, and caring. They make great friends and lovers.

ESFJ

The Consul Personality, these thoughtful individuals appreciate getting in touch with others as well as feeling close to them. They often seem far more like an open book than they genuinely are, keeping specific points hidden beneath the surface. This is mainly because ESFJs don't want to feel like a bother to those around them. These are strong, practical people who are sensitive to the needs of others. They don't want to be anybody's burden. Outgoing, organized, and tender-hearted, they make excellent care-takers.

ISTP

The Virtuoso Personality. ISTPs most definitely aren't open publications, mainly because they keep to themselves most of the time. Even their own parents may not be able to read them. ISTPs do not like to feel like they are hiding themselves; they simply do not naturally open themselves up because they are so introverted. ISTPs can be somewhat mystical individuals, keeping their thoughts and sensations to themselves most of the time because they are so focused on their inner world. They enjoy learning and perfecting their craft through careful application and performance. These are the artists of the world.

ESTP

The Entrepreneur. These energetic thrill seekers excel at putting out little fires everywhere. They are outgoing and action-oriented and often dramatic. What you see, however, may not be the real person. It is often smoke and mirrors. Appearances are important. That is how businesses succeed. Networking is everything. ESTPs generally have a wide circle of friends and acquaintants.

ISFP

The Adventurer Personality is, surprisingly, an introvert. He's so busy *doing* that he doesn't have time to expose his personality. He's observing the world. Living it. Feeling it with everything he's got. And that makes him/her a good parent. His cheerful, low-key, in-the-moment presence keeps him focused on care-taking even while he's active. So he/she is a good choice for parenting and partnering.

ESFP

The Entertainer Personality, ESFPs are most definitely open books that occasionally have a hard time keeping back their thoughts and feelings indeed. They are comfy showing themselves to those around them because this is what typically comes from them. ESFPs usually feel a deep demand to share themselves openly. This is simply part of who they are and not something they seek to change. They're outgoing, social entertainers who can be sensitive to criticism. Spontaneous, energetic creatures, they love to engage with those around them. Keep them in the social circle and close to family and friends.

Knowing these 16 Myers-Briggs Personality Types well will help you quickly summarize a person's personality when only knowing a little bit about them. It will help you to read them much more quickly and get a grip on who they are and what they are about.

CHAPTER 11: HOW TO ANALYZE THE TRUTHFULNESS IN A RELATIONSHIP

If there's something that will undoubtedly send your coupledom down in flames, it's lies and deceit. It doesn't matter if you're telling little white lies or great big whales tales -- your connection needs to be genuine to function. Honesty is what all the other good things are built on. If you do not believe this (or have convinced yourself otherwise), then think back to a time when you proved the fact. Even if you were simply lying about something small, the entire thing most likely spiraled out of control. Pretty soon you were slipping about, building on the lies, and needing to remember everything you said. You were tired, you might say, and points most likely got confused.

So why do we do it? Why do we make our lives more difficult, instead of merely spilling the beans? As Nicole Martinez, Psy.D., LCPC, tells me through e-mail, "Couples often tend to be unethical with each other for the same reasons that we are dishonest with any person. We want to avoid dispute, punishment, or anticipated misery."

It makes sense. And yet, attempting to prevent any kind of possible discomfort just makes things worse. It's much better to face the truth directly, and handle it as a pair. Below are some methods to do that, so you both can have a much healthier and more honest connection.

A lot of us agree that honesty is a basic structure on which to construct a partnership. Despite the terrific things we say regarding being straightforward -- that it's "the best policy" or that "the truth shall set us free" -- research informs us that we aren't so great at it.

According to researches by Bella DePaulo, individuals lie in 1 of 5 of their communications. These lies aren't just to unfamiliar people -- pairs regularly trick each other. DePaulo's study showed that dating couples lie to their partner a 3rd of the time, while married couples do so in as much as 1 in 10 interactions. While people seem to tell less of the "little white lies" to loved ones, 64% of our significant lies (deep disloyalties) do entail people's closest connection partners. Distinguished connection scientist John Gottman examined focus groups of pairs from around the nation and found that trust and dishonesty were one of the most vital issues to arise between partners.

Just how can we create more trust when we continue to lie to the people closest to us? Honesty is a vital component of a healthy partnership, not just because it aids us to stay clear of severe breaches of trust, but because it allows us to live instead of fantasize and to share this reality with another. Of course, every human has his/her unique understanding of the world; however, by sharing these understandings, we become familiar with each other for who we actually are. What can we do not only to be more honest but also to promote an atmosphere of sincerity around us? How can we generate a consistent circulation of truth-telling between ourselves and individuals we enjoy most? Commit to the following:

1. Know Yourself and Your Intentions.

To be truthful with somebody else, we must recognize ourselves first. We have to understand what we think and feel concerning the world around us. Frequently in life, we are either influenced by or adapting a collection of "shoulds" imposed on us by society, specifically the culture from which we originate. We might get married since everyone our age is "calming down." Or we may resist getting wed since our moms and dads never got along.

It is necessary to distinguish ourselves from unsafe impacts on our personality that don't mirror that we are as well as what we desire. If a voice in our head is informing us not to gamble or be prone, it's essential to doubt where those thoughts come from, after that align our actions to that which we need. This goes for all addictions – alcohol, drugs, pornography, whatever may call to us.

When we acknowledge ourselves by doing this, we are much more able to be sincere with the people around us. We are less likely to simply inform people of what they wish to hear or try to conceal aspects of ourselves of which we feel ashamed. Instead, we can be straightforward concerning who we are and what we want in a partnership.

2. Make Your Actions Match Your Words.

Make sure what you say is what you mean. Things like saying "I love you" or doing specific things together come to be a matter of routine rather than the passion that emerges from how we truly feel. When we create what my father, Robert Firestone, called a "dream bond" -- an impression of connection that replaces real, loving means of associating -- we frequently start to feel distant from our partner or lose interest. We may begin to make justifications for pulling away, or we may still talk of remaining in love while not participating in actions that are caring toward our companion.

To prevent this wrong way of relating, it is necessary to show stability continually and to make our activities match our words. If we say we are in love, we should take part in actions toward our partner that someone else would undoubtedly observe as loving. We must invest good, quality time with our companion, in which we slow down and make contact. We need to reveal our sensations, not merely in words but via our body language. Saying "I enjoy you," while grimacing or sighing at every step our companion makes, is not an expression of love that matches what we supposedly really feel.

3. Be Sincere Concerning Your Reactions.

Not everything we feel in a partnership will be cozy and also unclear. Yet, being honest and straight with somebody we love does not mean we need to be upsetting or harsh. Sharing life with a person, we are bound to discover some of their unfavorable tendencies and defenses that obstruct our feelings of closeness. When we aren't open with our partner concerning what we feel and see, we may grow cynical or begin constructing a situation versus them that, in fact, distorts and exaggerates their problems.

Rather than being overly critical or mad, we must aim to be open with our companion in revealing what we think and feel. We can say things like, "I miss you when you work all the time," or, "I feel much less drawn to you when you act hard or try to control what we do together." These honest, direct statements may feel uncomfortable sometimes. Still, they originate from an area of vulnerability and visibility that can bring about even more closeness and intimacy.

4. Be Open to Comments.

As well as we should be direct with our companion, we must also be open to hearing comments directed towards us. We need to pay attention to our partners and to see things from their perspective. What are they trying to tell us about how they are experiencing us and feeling towards us? Instead of arguing every small detail, we need to look for the kernel of truth in what our lover tells us. It is essential not to be defensive, reactive or penalizing in our responses. If we act victimized or crumble when we listen to criticism, then we psychologically adjust our companion and encourage them to sugarcoat or even lie to us in the future. Having a companion that feels comfortable to open to us is the best-case scenario for having a sincere partnership in which we can both fully grow and develop ourselves.

5. Approve Your Companion as a Separate Person.

No matter how connected we might feel to someone else, we will continuously be two different people with two sovereign minds. If our partner doesn't see things the same way we do, it does not necessarily mean we're incompatible. It just implies that we are two people who observe the world from different points of view. The more we accept this reality, the comfier we will be agree to disagree. By being honest with each other, we can recognize as well as accept each other for who we are, not what we wish each other to be. In this situation, neither one of us needs to make-believe to be someone else or attempt to fit a particular pre-conceived notion or assumption. We can accept each other for the important things that make us who we are as individuals, that light us up as well as offer our lives significance.

This willingness to be truthful, even when it's uncomfortable, helps establish reliability on each other and the relationship. An open dialogue, despite how hard it may feel, truly sets us free; we can accept that we are two individuals who choose to be together despite our differences. Most significantly, when we make this choice, we can rest assured that it's because we like each other and not just because we are attracted to the fantasy of being with each other.

Living honestly, things may not always have a fairytale ending, but as people, we are resilient. We can handle our partner feeling attracted to someone else, and we can manage to tell him or her when we feel insecure, afraid, or even furious. We can handle anything, as long as we are willing to live in reality and deal with the facts that exist. Honesty in partnerships makes us feel protected since we understand where we stand. When we are sincere with ourselves and our lover, we can experience the delight and exhilaration of living in an actual connection in which we are chosen for who we are.

6. Prepare To Face The Facts.

The most frightening part regarding being straightforward and sincere is recognizing the fact. If deceit has been afoot for a while, this might mean facing something you have been more than happy to sweep under the carpet. But try not to be afraid of what you'll learn. "Great or poor, it is a fact," Martinez says. If it doesn't tear you apart, it will bring you closer -- and that's sort of the point.

7. Talk About Problems When They Happen.

Crucial discussions should not be delayed, according to Scott Stabile on MindBodyGreen.com. So make a routine of talking about problems as they happen. He recommends allowing time for the conversation that helps both of you and sticking with it. Whether it's a simple misunderstanding, or substantial trouble, discussing it while it's fresh will protect against things spiraling out of control.

8. Be As Patient As Possible.

Occasionally being straightforward is very hard, and you might discover you're significant other is struggling for the appropriate words. If that is the case, carefully hear them out. "Nobody interacts completely. It is essential to be patient with your companion as they struggle to express themselves," Stabile said. "Listen to what they're saying with openness and perseverance." It'll make it simpler for both of you. Hopefully, they will, in turn, do the same for you.

9. Be Honest With Your Reactions.

If your companion is putting his or her heart out, you might be tempted to gaze back with a straight face, regardless of feeling mad, or distressed, or hurt. That may be the respectful thing to do, but it isn't specifically practical. If something they claim is genuinely rubbing you the wrong way, it's better to say so. (Done in the name of sincerity, right?).

Keep these suggestions in mind to bring sincerity, and closeness, into your relationship. Honesty is the best policy.

CHAPTER 12: HOW THE MIND COMMUNICATES

The word "telepathy" has been derived from the words "tele" implying distance and "pathy" implying sensation. So telepathy suggests getting sensations from a distance. To specify, telepathy is the communication between two minds, across a distance, without the use of the five known senses.

At some time or another, all of us have experienced telepathy. Perhaps you were thinking of a person you have not talked to in months, and you unexpectedly get a call from them. Or when two individuals are together, they say the very same thing at the same time. These are spontaneous mind-to-mind communications that tend to take place most often between closely related people. Right here are the steps:

Sender and Receiver

This requires two people. One will be the Sender who will attempt to transmit thoughts; the other will be the Receiver who will try to receive the ideas conveyed by the Sender. Before the experiment, make a decision plainly if you are going to be the Sender or the Receiver. If you do not, you both might wind up being Receivers or Senders! Avoid that complication. For this short section, we will think that you are the Sender.

Belief

First of all, it is very vital that the Sender and the Receiver both believe that telepathy is possible. Even if the idea is not 100%, an open-minded mindset is a must. It is best if the individuals not only rely on telepathy but genuinely prefer it to take place. If you are a skeptic, and if the doors of your mind are closed, you will have inferior outcomes.

Physical Relaxation

Telepathy is most effective when the Sender, and the Receiver, are both kicked back -literally. Likewise, remaining in favorable health and wellness makes you focus better. Try not to practice when you are unhealthy. Relax yourself using any relaxation method you prefer. You can either deeply or make use of a dynamic relaxation method.

Clear Your Mind

Clear your mind of unwanted thoughts. Make your mind tranquil. Let ideas occur, but don't hold on to them. Focus on your purpose. Considering that you are the Sender, your emphasis will be to send your thoughts across space. Your companion, the Receiver, needs to focus his mind to be open and responsive to your ideas.

See to it that both of you have no kind of distractions around. A disturbed setting will be harmful to your progress. A tranquil and quiet atmosphere will offer maximum results.

Visualization

Before starting the transmission, the previous steps must be well accomplished. They will set up the structure for your success. With your eyes shut, vividly picture the Receiver. Visualize that he is a couple of feet away from you. Visualize him in full color. Feel that he is there. If you desire, you can even view a colored picture of him before the experiment. This will certainly aid you to visualize him correctly. Envision a silver tube connecting your mind and his soul. This tube is the network where your thoughts will be connected to him. Picture this tube to be energetic. Know in your heart that this tube is handy and will certainly get the job done well. Please note that envisioning television is not a must. It is merely an efficient aid to help you to concentrate and provides your thoughts a distinct direction. Instead of this tube, you can picture that you are talking with your Receiver over the telephone or any other vivid visualization that helps you with your transmission.

Transmission

Visualize that your ideas are being sent via the tube - from your mind to his mind. If you are thinking of sending a mental picture of an apple, envision a great, red, juicy apple traveling through your tube (or other means of transmission). Make the picture as dazzling as possible. Fill the apple with emotion. Believe with all your possibility that telepathy is actual. Wish that your ideas reach your good friend. Envision the sensation you will have when you are successful. This is very critical. Emotions are a handy trigger as well as give excellent results. Usually, telepathy experiments stop working when the ideas lack psychological value. See to it you do not strain yourself to send out the thought. You need to be relaxed and composed.

When to End

While you are sending your ideas, there will undoubtedly be a minute when you will have a solid sensation that the thought has been transmitted. This is a distinct sensation that cannot be fabricated. Whenever you get such a feeling, the task is done. This may take a few seconds to many minutes. If after 15 minutes, you do not feel this sensation, you can abandon the experiment and attempt it again at a later time. Trying harder will certainly not help much since your mind would be tired.

The Receiver

Throughout the experiment, the Receiver should keep his mind blank and should attempt to receive the thoughts being sent by you. He needs to avoid trying too hard. Requiring himself to notice what you are thinking will undoubtedly sabotage your efforts. His mind will be most receptive when he is relaxed and at ease. He will get numerous impressions on his mind. He ought to keep a pen and paper next to him and take down whatever thoughts drift through his mind. He will probably feel that he is making things up. That's ok. This is how telepathy works.

Compare Outcomes

As soon as you are through with your experiments, compare your results. Inspect all the perceptions that the Receiver has made a note of. Does it consist of the idea that you tried to transfer? The more you practice, the more precise outcomes you will certainly obtain.

Repeat the Experiment

You ought to duplicate the experiment - either right away or at a later date. If you have obtained some success, your self-confidence will be quite high and you will certainly intend to repeat it instantly. However, if there was no success, do not let that prevent you from attempting it again the following day. Standard practice is a must because uniformity will undoubtedly make you much better. You ought to also alternate between being the Receiver and the Sender. This will certainly tell you what you are better at - receiving or rending.

Keep It Short

Keep your experiments short, maybe 15 minutes or less. This will protect against monotony and exhaustion. Your telepathic ability is at its top when you feel most energetic.

Persevere

One of the most crucial problems of speculative telepathic work is persistence. Don't be discouraged if you do not find much success initially. Any psychic experiment, including telepathy, takes some practice before you see outcomes. Once you practice for a few days, you will begin getting some successes.

Stay Away From Sceptics.

Doubters have obtained one purpose in life: to avert followers. Steer clear of such people because they will place uncertainty in your mind and will undoubtedly dampen your spirits. Your results prove to you that telepathy works. Doubters will certainly not help you much. Sharing your outcomes with them will only inhibit and prevent your success. Only share your experiences with like-minded people, people that share and encourage your endeavor.

CHAPTER 13: THE CONSCIOUS MIND

"The Fundamental Concept of the Mind" is a concept regarding the mind and its phenomena, such as awareness and individual experiences of conscious experience. It additionally entails related matters including the essential issue of consciousness, the explanatory space, variable qualia, p-zombies, and free choice. This theory is scientifically proven -- it is based on physical evidence and has experimentally testable forecasts.

The Mind

The mind is something that has continuously interested as well as puzzled us. It is the only point that we can be sure of existing, yet we do not know precisely what it is, why, or how it functions. This remains in comparison to things outside the mind, such as houses, cars, and trucks, and even other individuals, which we can not be certain that they exist -- they may just be illusions.

Further, the phenomena of qualia (defined as individual instances of subjective, conscious experience) and consciousness, such as the red shade as it appears phenomenally red in our mind and our extraordinarily aware awareness and experience of that red color, have always been baffling -- what is their nature, why and just how do they happen, and can there be only the mind without them?

The good news is, with centuries of studying these matters, (first by philosophers and later by neurologists, neuroscientists, and various other scientists in related areas) we currently have a wealth of scientific proof and concepts that are complete enough to create a theory that can address these fantastic problems. In Sigmund Freud's psychoanalytic theory of character, the aware mind contains everything inside of our recognition. This is the aspect of our mental handling that we can assume and speak about in a sensible method. The mindful mind consists of such things as the feelings, assumptions, memories, sensations, and fantasies within our current understanding. Very closely allied with the mindful mind is the preconscious (or subconscious), which includes the things that we are not thinking of at the moment, however, which we can quickly move into conscious recognition. Items that are in the unconscious are readily available to the conscious mind in a masked form. For instance, the contents of the psyche might spill right into recognition in the way of dreams. Freud believed that by assessing the content of dreams, individuals could find the unconscious influences on their aware actions.

The Aware Mind Is Just the Tip of the Iceberg

Freud often utilized the allegory of an iceberg to define the two major elements of human personality. The tip of the iceberg that extends above the water stands for the mindful mind. Underneath the water is the much larger bulk of the iceberg, which represents the unconscious. While the aware and preconscious is important, Freud believed that they were far less crucial than the unconscious. Things that are hidden from understanding, he thought, applied the most significant influence over our characters and habits.

How did the human mind arise from the collection of neurons that composes the mind? How did the brain acquire self-awareness, useful freedom, language, and the ability to believe, to understand itself, and the world? In this capacity in the Essential Knowledge series, Zoltan Torey uses an accessible and concise summary of the evolutionary breakthrough that developed the human mind.

Drawing on understandings from transformative biology, neuroscience, and linguistics, Torey rebuilds the series of occasions through which homo erectus came to be humankind. He defines the enhanced operating that underpins the emergent mind -- a brand-new ("off-line") internal feedback system with which the brain accesses itself and then develops a choice device for psychologically generated action options. This practical innovation, Torey says, clarifies how the animal mind's "recognition" ended up being self-accessible and reflective -- that is, just how the human brain got a mindful mind. Awareness, unlike animal recognition, is not a unitary sensation but a composite procedure. Torey's account shows how protolanguage progressed into language, how a brain subsystem for the rising mind was developed, as well as why these developments are opaque to self-questioning. We experience the brain's functional freedom, he suggests, as free choice.

Torey proposes that once life began, awareness had to arise -- because knowledge is the informational source of the brain's behavioral feedback. Consciousness, he argues, is not a newly acquired "top quality," "cosmic concept," "circuitry plan," or "epiphenomenon", as others have argued, but a crucial working component of the living system's fashion of working.

Conscious vs. Preconscious Differences

The aware mind includes every one of the things that you are presently mindful of and thinking of. It is somewhat similar to short-term memory and is limited in regards to ability. Your recognition of yourself and the world around you is part of your awareness. The preconscious mind, also known as the subconscious mind, consists of things that we could not be presently knowledgeable of but that we can draw right into conscious awareness when required. You may not currently be considering how to do long division, however, you can access the information and bring it into aware understanding when you are confronted with a math issue. The preconscious mind is a part of the brain that corresponds to average memory. These memories are not aware, yet we can bring them to mindful awareness at any time. If you were asked what television reveal you viewed last night or what you had for breakfast this morning, you would be drawing that information out of your preconscious.

In Freud's iceberg metaphor, the preconscious exists just below the surface of the water. You can see the murky shape and outline of the submerged ice if you focus and make an effort to view it. Like the unconscious mind, Freud believed that the preconscious could have an impact on mindful recognition. In some cases information from the preconscious surfaces in unforeseen ways, like in dreams or unintentional slips of the tongue (referred to as Freudian slides). While we might not be proactively thinking about these points, Freud believed they still served to influence mindful actions and behaviors.

The more you know about how the mind works, the better able you will be at understanding how another person thinks. That will allow you to 'step into' their thoughts, to understand what motivates them, to empathize with them. Analyzing them will then be a piece of cake.

CHAPTER 14: THE SUBCONSCIOUS MIND

Your subconscious mind has something called a homeostatic impulse, which manages functions like body temperature level, heartbeat, and breathing. Brian Tracy (Subconscious Mind Power Explained) described it like this: "Your autonomic nervous system, [your homeostatic impulse] maintains the balance among the hundreds of chemicals in your billions of cells so that your entire physical machine functions in complete harmony most of the time."

Yet what many people do not understand is that just as your brain is developed to regulate your physical self, so does it try to control your mental self. Your mind is the regularly filtering system offering you interesting information as well as stimulations that affirm your pre-existing ideas (this is recognized in psychology as confirmation prejudice) in addition to presenting you with duplicated thoughts and impulses that resemble and mirror that which you've carried out in the past.

1. Agree to See the Opportunity.

The primary step in developing substantial change in your life is to think that it's possible. But your mind is firstly a doubter. You are not likely to be able to leap from being a complete doubter to a steadfast believer. The step between those merely is being open to seeing what is feasible. You can attempt sending out a couple of "frightening emails," in which you suggest a customer or companion do something. You might have a few ignored messages, yet at some point, someone will respond. The point is that you're willing to see if it's possible. That creates doubt and opens up possibilities and points you in the right direction. You have moved from Defeatist Mode to Opportunity Mode. That's what will alter your life. Now move forward.

2. Offer Your Permission to be Effective.

Rather than throwing up the usual story of believing you'll be more than happy when you're 10 pounds lighter, one promotion, and two life occasions down-the-line, work on changing your stream of consciousness to: "I allow my life to be great."

Provide your approval to be delighted and successful, and not feel guilty concerning it. If you have a subconscious feeling that success is amoral, or corrupt, obviously you're not going to do what you need to do to live the life you wish to live. Instead, give yourself permission to enter a whole, satisfied, healthy life that is significant in its presence.

3. Don't Allow Other People's Worries to Cast Shadows of Doubt.

The method people respond to news of your success will certainly inform you how they are doing in their lives. If you introduce your fiancé, individuals who are in satisfying marital relationships will undoubtedly be happy for you. People who remain in unhappy marriages will undoubtedly advise you that it is difficult and that you should enjoy your time as "single" individuals. The point is that individuals' worries are forecasts of their situations. They have nothing to do with what you are or aren't capable of. So don't let other people's opinions of their lives influence your feelings on your own life.

4. Surround Yourself with Favorable Support.

Maintain a bottle of sparkling wine in the fridge. Modify your early morning alarm on your phone to check out the message: "CONGRATULATIONS!!!" Ensure that the items that you see and touch most often bring you positivity and hopefulness. Maintain an inspirational note on a post-it next to your computer system. Unfollow people who make you feel poorly concerning yourself and follow those who are regularly posting motivational messages and exciting concepts. Make your newsfeed a place that can catalyze your growth, as opposed to reducing your assumption of your worth. All of these things will uplift you and help you maintain a positive self-attitude.

5. Speak Your Success as Real Truth, Not a Plan.

Though you shouldn't state points like "I drive a Ferrari," or "I am a CEO," if they are not true, do begin speaking about what it is you want out of life, not in the context that you will one day have it, but as if you are already living it. Rather than saying: "I wish to do that one day," claim, "I am planning exactly how to do that now." Rather than thinking, "I will be happy when I am in another place in my life," believe, "I am entirely capable of enjoying right here and now, nothing is holding me back."

6. Produce a Vision Board.

Being able to picture what it is you desire out of your life is necessary for developing it since if you don't understand where you're going, you won't know which way to turn. Once you have a crystal clear photo in your mind for what it is you desire and how it is you want to live, you then can develop it. If you are still hazy or torn about what you desire, you will be rendered incapable of making actual, meaningful plans toward it. Whether you use a Pinterest board, blog site, note pad, or bulletin board, put together words and pictures that represent what you envision and how you want to live.

7. Recognize Your Resistance.

When our subconscious minds hold us back from going after something that we love, it is because we are holding a different belief regarding it. To recognize your resistance, query yourself. Ask yourself why you feel better when you procrastinate, or why obtaining what you want can put you in a place that makes you feel more vulnerable than ever before. Discover a way to placate that fear before you proceed. Use mindfulness techniques to soothe yourself. Visualize yourself as calm. Then visualize yourself as powering through your fear to opportunity and success.

8. Have a Master Plan for Your Life.

Forget five and even ten-year strategies; so many changes gradually; it's difficult to establish objectives that you'll be able to maintain. Probably new or perhaps much better chances will surface, and though your life will not look like you thought it would certainly, you're much better off for that. Instead, have a master plan. Determine your core worths and inspirations. Ask yourself what is the supreme objective of what you want to accomplish while you live; picture the sort of legacy you intend to leave. Once you have your Big Picture values recognized, you can make decisions for the long-term that align with your true self.

9. Begin a Gratitude Journal.

The very best way to begin putting yourself in a headspace of "having" as opposed to "wanting" is to start a thankfulness practice. By expressing thanks for all that you do have, you change your mindset from being starving for change to feeling completely satisfied with where you are. Nothing allures abundance to you like gratefulness. There's a saying that as soon as you believe you have enough, you are open to receiving more. That is certainly real.

10. Begin Asking for What You Desire, Even if You Understand You'll be Rejected.

If somebody asks you to do a consulting job, request the quantity of money you want to earn for it. If your objective is to get a promotion in your organization, take a seat with your employer and make your goals recognized. Connect to brands you wish to deal with. Begin asking for what you want, even if you have no reason to think that anyone will give you any one of those points. Ultimately, they will. Because you're worth it. Most of the time, people don't get what they want because they are simply afraid to ask for it.

11. Release Your Attachment to "Exactly How."

Your work is to determine what, then be flexible as to just how. If your goal is to function from another location and run your own business, instead of giving up if your initial effort falls short, attempt reimagining how else you can accomplish your ultimate goal in a new way that is more economically lucrative. The fact is that life will always amaze you with exactly how things evolve. Instead of being obsessively connected to every little detail happening the way you think it should, be open to possibility and opportunity, even if it's something you never envisioned.

12. Surround Yourself with Allies.

Start spending quality time with people who inspire, are supportive, and creative. If you're hanging around every weekend with people who are dissatisfied with their lives, you aren't likely to receive a wealth of support if you try to do your own thing. Keep in mind that you will become who you invest the most time with, and choose who that is carefully.

13. Fill your "Quiet" Time with Affirmation and Motivation.

When you're on your commute early each morning, listen to an inspirational speech or podcast. While you're doing the dishes or driving, tune into a talk show that connects to the sort of business you're interested in. Infuse your life with as much affirmation and inspiration as possible. You might need to listen to the lessons more than once, but they will leak into your mind with time, and ultimately, you will undoubtedly find yourself acting upon knowledge obtained from those that are where you wish to be.

The subconscious is tricky. But it is the subconscious that gives us the body cues which we can read in another person that they don't even know they are revealing. Understanding how the subconscious mind works once again gives you hidden insight into another person which can help you understand how they might be thinking without having to even speak to them. Simply observe. Your understanding of the inner workings of the mind will reveal much. After reading this chapter, you are much better prepared for this analysis.

CHAPTER 15: BENEFITS OF PERSONALITY ANALYSIS

Personality and aptitude tests (psychometrics) are useful for managing individuals and overlooking yourself. You ought to consider utilizing personality and inclination tests to select and hire people. Although the types and personality arrangement differ from test to test, they give insight into the human mind. There is a general inclination that numerous businesses are not utilizing the PAT (Personality Assessment Tests) after enrolling.

Costs: Most bosses feel the expense of overseeing these tests is above their financial limit. Some are unreasonably expensive to incorporate, thus constraining their use.

Information on the Advantages: Most bosses are uninformed of the benefits of PAT. This keeps them from being used. Most of these tests must be directed. Most potential workers might not be comfortable on the internet, although they should be by now, or a few bosses don't have network introduced in their workplaces. This constrains the number of workers with access to PAT.

Shady Contracting Practices: Some associations have not created or adjusted to the accepted procedures for employing. The techniques utilized are equivocal, and this constrains the utilization of PAT with numerous businesses.

PAT can help you avoid hiring employees who can damage your business with incompatible personalities. The cost is justified when fully employed.

CHAPTER 16: HOW BODY LANGUAGE IMPROVES YOUR MINDSET

Our body language is the way we speak with our outside world – most of us don't even realize we are doing it! Body language phenomenally affects the presentation of who you are as an individual. It impacts our posture and physiological wellbeing, yet it can change our psychological viewpoint, our impression of the world, and others' perception of us.

How Our Body Imparts

We use our body language to communicate our musings, thoughts, feelings; we synchronize body movements to the words that we express. We convey purposefully through activities like shrugging our shoulders or applauding just as we inadvertently say so much by twisting in on ourselves or pointing our feet toward the individual we are speaking with.

Before spoken language was created, our body language was the primary technique for communicating. Our body is our major method to speak in life!

How Can It Influence Our State of Mind?

Our body language is the way that we interface with the outside world. It is also the way that we associate with ourselves. How would you treat yourself? Do you slouch over when you walk, or do you walk tall and proud? Are you thankful for each task that your body does for you? Probably not; we regularly underestimate our body; we frequently neglect it. Body language can impact our physical body and posture. And it can change how we are feeling. Having a great attitude can affect attitude and causes us to have elevated levels of confidence and energy when we are confronted with pressure.

An up and coming field of psychology, known as mind-body therapy, asserts that the association between our body and our general surroundings doesn't merely impact us, it is woven into the way that we think. Studies in this field show that the individuals who are sitting in a hard seat are less inclined to bargain than those sitting in a delicate chair, and those holding warm beverages saw others as more mindful and liberal than those holding cold drinks. This examination shows that body language is a two-way road prompting both the outside and inward world.

Four Different Ways You Can Change Your Body Language

You can change your body language. It just takes a conscious effort.

Flip Around That Glare!

Grinning and snickering is infectious! A complete report on smiling found that a grin that draws in the mouth and moves the skin around the eyes can enact the cerebrum to experience positive feelings. So grin and grin frequently! Regardless of whether you are having an awful day, grin! It may very well help turn your day around!

Crossing Your Arms

Crossing the arms is a resistance system to protect the heart and lungs. We regularly do it when we feel shaky, anxious, or disturbed. The physical obstruction gives others the feeling that we are cut off and detached from them.

Crossing the arms is considered to be an antagonistic body posture. Some studies have indicated that crossing the arms can cause previously industrious people to feel like slowing down or stopping.

Simply uncrossing your arms may put you back in the mindset of working.

Positive Presenting

One of the significant specialists in the area of body language is Amy Cuddy. In her TedTalk, Cuddy talks about how body language can be the difference between succeeding and coming up short at prospective employee interviews. She made members pose in positive stances and negative poses for two minutes before sending them into an interview. She estimated levels of the pressure hormone cortisol and the predominance hormone testosterone. The outcomes demonstrated that those remaining in positive stances had expanded degrees of testosterone and lower levels of cortisol than those in negative poses.

Quit Slumping

This may appear glaringly evident, however, slumping doesn't only influence your spine, it can likewise change your state of mind! Indeed, slumping can cause back pain and an irregular spine arrangement. Intellectually, it can leave you feeling miserable, lacking vitality, and shut off from others. Sitting and standing up straighter can help with settling back torment as well as lift your attitude and state of mind.

Changing your posture can be trying for your body at first, particularly if you are accustomed to slumping over for long periods. You may feel muscle pain in the neck, back, and buttocks – don't stress, this will pass. Meanwhile, I'd suggest utilizing Atrogel, a natural relief from discomfort cure containing concentrates of arnica blossoms.

Improve Your Posture to Improve Your Temperament!

Body language isn't the first thing you'd think of when you are experiencing a low state of mind, however, investigating our body language can reveal how we are truly feeling. Our body language has an immediate connection to our temperament, similarly, our mindset influences our posture.

Simple Ways You Can Fix Your Posture to Adjust Your State of Mind:

- Smile when you are having a terrible day!
- Unfold your arms when you feel anxious and permit yourself to be open to circumstances.
- Turning the palms of your hands forward when you walk will urge the shoulders to unwind back as opposed to slumping forward.
- Power present before high-pressure situations like prospective employer interviews.

Body Language Signs When Someone Hides Something From You

Untrustworthiness. It happens in many connections – and a great deal of the time, it accomplishes more mischief than anything. Even in intimate relationships, lies happen. But it is best to be honest. Lying in such a close relationship shows that you don't regard your partner enough to recognize that they are deserving of the truth. You are saying that they aren't important enough to be given what's genuine – and that is, in every case, terrible in a relationship. You generally need to confess all to your partner, particularly about vital issues encompassing your relationship.

Still, many of us are childish. Reality can be difficult to stomach. We are afraid of the consequences of the truth, not thinking of the worse results of a lie being uncovered. So we choose to lie to delay consequences.

That is hazardous for a relationship. You can't hope to make your connection work appropriately if you're not taking care of the best possible realities. You generally need to ensure that you know all that is going on, so you don't wind up getting tricked or bushwhacked by anything.

Men aren't generally the best verbal communicators. You may already know this. But the truth may be communicated through his body language. He may disclose to you a lot of things about himself without meaning to through his posture. You simply need to spot the signs when they present themselves. You need to ensure that you pay attention to things in your relationship. Here are some essential body language signs that your man is concealing something from you.

1. He Crosses His Arms When He Talks to You.

He may not see that he's doing it. He's subliminally folding his arms since he's attempting to hide something. He wouldn't like to give you access to everything. He's shutting himself off to you in a specific way. And that is the reason he's utilizing his arms as a boundary.

2. He Does Not Face His Body Towards You When You're Talking.

It's conspicuous that he is attempting to conceal something if his body shifts in another direction when he's conversing with you. Rather than utilizing his arms as a method of safeguard, he just totally closes the entryway on you by dismissing you and facing in the other direction.

3. He Avoids Eye Contact During Conversation.

He doesn't need you to see the dread in his eyes. He doesn't want you to see reality by looking straight into his soul. The eyes are the windows to the soul.

4. He is Easily Irritated When You Ask Him Questions.

He gets guarded when you ask him necessary questions about his life. He is going to make it seem as though you're investigating him when you're not. The weight is beginning to get to him, and he's going to act extremely irritated. He wouldn't like to get trapped in his falsehoods.

5. He Gets Fidgety When It's Just the Two of You Alone.

He is eager. The mystery is genuinely squeezing him. There's such a significant amount of vitality within him that he needs to discharge it in one way or another. He needs to diminish the entirety of that pressure. That is the reason he will experience issues with keeping still.

6. He Tries to Keep a Blank Expression on His Face All the Time.

He has a poker face on. Also, he's undoubtedly attempting to hide something – much like in poker. He doesn't need you to recognize what cards he's holding. He's keeping his cards hidden from everyone else, and he's under a great deal of pressure.

7. He Acts Like a Blinking Machine.

Brain research has demonstrated that individuals who are lying or who are keeping mysteries will, in general, blink at a quick rate. So be careful about the recurrence of his blinking.

8. He Bites His Fingernails.

Brain research has additionally expressed that the demonstration of gnawing fingernails is an indication of uncertainty or nervousness. On the off chance that he's restless about the mystery he's stowing away, he will be chewing his fingernails a great deal. Of course, for some people, this is just a nervous habit they do all the time.**9. He Lashes Out at You a Lot.**

He is so blameworthy about the mystery that he's stowing away. He realizes that it's inappropriate to keep something from you. The blame is beginning to gobble him up inside. Also, he's attempting to carry on despite the blame. He will reverse the situation on you and cause it to appear as though you're the person who is hiding something. It's called projecting. Of course, he could just be a real jerk. That's for you to determine.

Getting and Understanding Nonverbal Signals

The Most Effective Method to Read Negative Body Language

Monitoring negative body language in others can permit you to understand implicit issues or awful emotions. Along these lines, we'll feature some negative nonverbal signs that you should pay attention to.

Troublesome Conversations and Defensiveness

Troublesome or tense discussions are an awkward unavoidable part of life. Maybe you've needed to manage an annoying client, or expected to converse with somebody about their terrible showing. Then again, perhaps you've arranged an important agreement.

In a perfect world, these circumstances would be settled calmly. Often, they are entangled by feelings of apprehension, stress, contrariness, or even resentment. However we may attempt to shroud them, these feelings regularly appear through our body language. For instance, on the chance that somebody is showing at least one of the accompanying movements, he will probably be withdrawn, uninvolved, or miserable:

- Arms collapsed before the body.
- Insignificant or tense outward appearance.
- The body some distance away from you, more than in a normal conversation.
- Eyes averted, seldom connecting touch.
- Keeping away from Unengaged Audiences.

At the point when you have to convey an introduction or to work together in a gathering, you need the individuals around you to be 100% locked in. Here are some "obvious" signs that individuals might be exhausted or biased to what you're stating:

- Sitting drooped, with heads sad.
- Looking at something different, or into space.
- Squirming, picking at garments, or tinkering with pens and telephones.
- Composing or doodling.

Step by step instructions to Project Positive Body Language:

When you use positive body language, it can add solidarity to the verbal messages or thoughts that you need to convey and help you to abstain from imparting blended or befuddling signs. In this segment, we'll portray some fundamental postures that you can embrace to extend fearlessness and receptiveness.

Establishing a Confident First Connection

These tips can assist you in adjusting your body language, so you establish a positive first connection:

Have an Open Posture. Be loose, but, don't slump! Sit or stand straight and place your hands by your sides. Resist putting your hands on your hips, as this will cause you to seem more aggressive, which can convey animosity or a craving to rule.

Use a Firm Handshake. However, don't become overly energetic! You don't need to get unbalanced or, worse, excruciating for the other person. On the chance that it does, you'll likely seem to be impolite or overly aggressive.

Keep in Touch. Try to maintain eye contact with the other person for a couple of seconds one after another. This will convey that you're connected and locked in. However, abstain from turning it into a staring contest.

Resist Touching Your Face. There's a typical perception that people who touch their face while answering questions are being untrustworthy. While this isn't always the case, it's preferable to abstain from fussing with your hair or touching your mouth or nose, especially if your point is to meant to be taking seriously.

Public Speaking

Positive body language can help you when engaging individuals, to hide introduction nerves, and to create an aura of confidence when public speaking. Follow these tips.

Have a Positive Posture. Sit or stand upright with your shoulders back and your arms unfurled and at your sides or before you. Try to keep your hands out of your pockets, and resist slumping, as this will make you look disinterested.

Keep Your Head Up. Your head ought to be upright and level. Hanging downward or tilted back excessively can make you look forceful or self-important.

Practice Impeccable Posture. You'd practice your introduction in advance, so why not practice your body language as well? Remain casual with your weight equally distributed. Keep one foot slightly before the other – this will assist you with maintaining your posture. Think 'first position' for those who know a bit about ballet.

Utilize Open Hand Motions. Keep your hands separated, before you, with your palms marginally toward your crowd. This demonstrates an ability to convey and share thoughts. Keep your upper arms near your body. Take care to avoid over gesturing or individuals may give more consideration to your hands than to what you're stating.

CONCLUSION

Personality analysis from body language is an art. And having positive body language is a blessing. Hence, it's essential to have appropriate body development and posture while talking in front of an audience before a crowd of people.

Body language is significant in all types of interactions. It assists with breaking the obstruction of newness and assists with shaping a superior interface without the beneficiary of data. Understanding body language can go far toward helping you better speak with others and deciphering what others may be attempting to pass on to you or hide from you.

While it might be enticing to dissect flags individually, it's critical to take a look at these nonverbal signals within verbal correspondence, other nonverbal signs, and the circumstance.

MIND MASTERY SERIES

SECRET MANIPULATION TECHNIQUES

How Subliminal Psychology Can Persuade Anyone by Applying Dark PNL in Real-Life. Understanding Tactics & Schemes to Influence People and Control Their Emotions

HOW TO SPEED READ PEOPLE

Reading Human Body Language To Understand Psychology And Dark Side Of The Persons – How To Analyze Behavioral Emotional Intelligence For The Mind Control

NLP MASTERY

How To Analyze Dark Psychology Techniques To Change Your Habits And Build A Successful Life. Essential Guide On Mind Control Through Calibrating Emotional Intelligence And Hidden Emotions

EMOTIONAL INTELLIGENCE MASTERY

Discover How EQ Can Make You More Productive At Work And Strengthen Relationship. Improve Your Leadership Skills To Analyze & Understand Other People Through Empathy

*"For better enjoyment, you CAN find all this titles also in audio format, on **Audible.**"*

MY FREE STEP-BY-STEP HELP

I'll send you a free eBook! Yes, you got it right! I'll send you my future projects, in preview, with nothing in return, if you just write a realistic review on them, which I'm sure will be useful to me. Thanks in advance!

Leave me your best email. My staff will send you a copy as soon as possible:

liamrobinsonauthor@gmail.com

Do not go yet; One last thing to do…

*If you enjoyed this book or found it useful, I'd be very grateful if you'd post a short review on **Amazon**. Your support really does make a difference and I read all the reviews personally so I can get your feedback and make this book even better.*

Thanks again for your support!

© Copyright 2020 by **LIAM ROBINSON**

All rights reserved

Made in the USA
Middletown, DE
08 December 2021